MW01073160

A FEW DAYS IN ATHENS

A FEW DAYS IN ATHENS

By Frances Wright; Commentary by Hiram Crespo

This work is in the public domain. Feel free to copy and share for educational purposes.

ISBN-13: 978-1507709061
ISBN-10: 1507709064

In Praise of Frances Wright

The first thing I told myself after reading *A Few Days in Athens* is "Why did I wait so long to read this masterpiece?". That was the same reaction I had to reading Lucian's Alexander the Oracle-Monger, a work which I knew about for very long but had been too lazy to read, and I even felt the need to apologize to our predecessor by writing a piece <u>in praise of Lucian</u>. Let this be my piece in praise of Frances Wright, as this is perhaps the only extant work by a female Epicurean author advocating in no uncertain terms a return to the wisdom of Epicurus.

The work had been recommended to me by Cassius, who has a page dedicated to it at <u>newepicurean.com</u>, and who has said the following:

> *It is an amazing piece of material … It probably qualifies as the real (Epicurean) "Atlas Shrugged" or ultimate English-language manifesto of Epicurean philosophy, and it also lends itself to almost being used–without any changes at all–for a modern movie or screenplay that could easily be staged … I believe the portrayal of*

doctrine to be 100% faithful ... Almost all the minute episodes and references are from various books of Diogenes Laertius, but the material is combined and told in story-form in such a way as to be a work of genius.

In general, I find the book extremely faithful to the core texts on every core point. And virtually every aspect of the book is a helpful explanation of Epicurean doctrine, along with a comparison of how he differed from other philosophers.

Short of Epicurus' own letters, and Lucretius, and Diogenes of Oinoada, this is probably THE undiscovered treasure of world Epicurean literature. I am not familiar with what has been published in other languages, but it really stands alone in the English world, at least.

Simply by reading this one, single, easy-and-fun-to-read book, any educated layman can have a better grasp of the core ideas of Epicurus than most college students have after four years and a degree in philosophy.

Cassius also expresses doubts as to whether a young Frances Wright wrote the work by herself or with the aid of her great-uncle

James Mylne, a professor of moral philosophy at Glasgow College who mentored her during a period of her life, as she was an orphan and moved to live with him in Scotland when she was 21. We can't make any definite claims of co-authorship by her uncle, but he would have had a reputation to uphold, and with this being a book written partly in defense of atheism, it's fair to consider the possibility of co-authorship.

I personally do not doubt that she could have written the work entirely by herself. She was a brilliant, passionate woman with very progressive views who (according to the sources) was acquainted with French materialist philosophy from an early age (a tradition which originates, let us not forget, with Pierre Gassendi: an Epicurean) and later went on to become a secularist, feminist and abolitionist activist, as well as one of Susan B. Anthony's personal heroes.

A Few Days in Athens was also personally recommended by Thomas Jefferson and Marquis de Lafayette.

A treat to me of the highest order. The

matter and manner of the dialogue is strictly ancient ... the scenery and portraiture of the interlocutors are of higher finish than anything in that line left us by the ancients; and like Ossian, if not ancient, it is equal to the best morsels of antiquity. – Thomas Jefferson

... which should lead us to consider the historical importance of this work and its author. Together with Lafayette, Wright is known to have spent some time in the company of Thomas Jefferson when she came to America, an event which led to her humanitarian plan to purchase, educate, and later emancipate slaves. She scandalously criticized racial segregation more than a century prior to its abolition and called for miscegenation: the cultural and sexual mixing of races. She also exchanged letters with Jefferson, and shared with him an outspoken, profound distrust of the central bank.

As an interesting side note, which is reminiscent of the suspicion aroused by Epicurus' early and precocious treatment of women as intellectual equals: the relationship between Lafayette and Wright also attracted gossip, and she even suggested he legally adopt her in order to silence the dissenting voices. It seems that Lafayette considered her worthy of meeting the other great minds of her day. So rare were the instances of women being treated as intellectual equals. It's a testament to Epicureanism's progressive values that our tradition nurtured these egalitarian models (invariably enduring gossip as it did so) 2,400 years ago, and then again a couple of hundred years ago.

It's possible that A Few Days in Athens (which was written at the insistence of her co-conspirator Lafayette) is the novel that converted the founding father to Epicureanism, and in fact Jefferson carried around a notebook with quotes from the book.

Cassius also attests as to how complete an education in Epicureanism just reading this book represents, which makes is therefore a must-read for everyone studying our tradition and wanting to get a grasp of it on its own terms.

One thing this book NAILS DOWN is that

(Jefferson) was not just some generic deist who had vague anti-christian feelings. This books shows (because it contains) that he was fully conversant in the most intricate details of the debates between the ancient schools, so when he said "I too am an Epicurean" he was not just talking loosely — he would have had a full understanding of what that meant.

Overview of the Work

Enough drum-beating! Let us now turn to a discussion of the book itself. The work commences with a claim of being a translation of a manuscript found in Herculaneum, but this reference was fictional and meant as a literary device.

The only set of views that is a later development in Epicureanism is Frances' apparent agnosticism, which contrasts with the piety of the original founders of our tradition. This sympathy with atheistic views even takes on a strident tone reminiscent of contemporaries like Richard Dawkins and (Epicurean author) Christopher Hitchens at the point towards the end of the novel where religion is even denominated the root of all evil.

> *I have found the first link in the chain of evil; I have found it–in all countries–among all tribes and tongues and nations; I have found it, Fellow-men, I have found it in RELIGION.*
>
> *We have named the leading error of the human mind, the bane of human happiness, the perverter of human virtue! It is RELIGION, that dark coinage of trembling ignorance! That poisoner of human felicity! That blind guide of human reason! That dethroner of human virtue which lies at the root of all evil and all the misery that pervade the world!*

We must treat Wright as an independent mind with an independent history and interpretation of Epicureanism. Just as Simone de Beauvoir was the feminist counterpart to Sartre among the French existentialists, Wright may be seen as an insightful feminist who is much less forgiving of religion than men (who have always enjoyed–even if at times unaware–religion's privileges) may be inclined to be. Frances Wright's Epicureanism is not the Epicureanism of our founders. It is a much freer, contemporary version of our tradition, one that could have only flourished where dissent does not necessarily invite danger.

Yet, this Epicureanism retains its refined, polished quality, and even fills the heart with love of virtue. Sages are viewed as compassionate, playful and just; the innocence of the good is justly protected and insisted upon, as there can be no imperturbability without innocence; good manners and wholesome character are celebrated.

> *If I ever saw simple, unadorned goodness; If I ever heard simple, unadorned truth, it is in, it is from Epicurus.*

The book *A Few Days in Athens* is itself an exercise in good association and leaves us with the accompanying after-glow. One can easily envision and experience the healthy effects of associating with the virtuous, and one ends up wishing to profit from the study at the feet of philosophy–who is personified and even speaks in the first person, as in other wisdom traditions, in a section of the book.

Proper Relation Between Master and Pupil

The Stoic master Zeno and our own, Epicurus, are seen throughout the book as Guru figures. In a manner somewhat reminiscent of the Eastern protocol for relations between guru (spiritual teacher) and chela (pupil), here the pupil must be ready and receptive to the instructor and to the teaching in order to profit from the relationship.

> *Teach me, guide me, make me what you will. My soul is in your hand. – Theon, taking refuge in Epicurus in A Few Days in Athens*

On the other hand, reciprocity is expected and the Guru must be worthy of the name and lead by example. It's understood that Epicurus taught by example and that his life is his message.

> *I answer (Stoic lies) with my life. – Epicurus, in A Few Days in Athens*

Epicureans in antiquity believed that true sages taught philosophy by embodying the virtues so thoroughly that their mere presence had an effect on pupils. A similar belief exists also in the East, where the vision of a saint (called darshan), either in dream or awakened state, is considered a huge blessing. Wright's book contains a detailed description of the main woman philosopher from the original Garden, Leontion. She is depicted as being comparable to Athena in dignity, wisdom and demeanor.

Throughout the text Epicurus is depicted as mild and candid. The author places words of praise for Epicurus and his virtues on the lips of Metrodorus, again evoking a sense of darshan:

> *The life of Epicurus is a lesson of wisdom. It is by example, even more than precept, that he guides his disciples. Without issuing commands, he rules despotically ... We are a family of brothers, of which Epicurus is the father.*
>
> *Many of us have had bad habits, many of us evil propensities, violent passions. That our habits are corrected, our propensities changed, our passions restrained, lies all with Epicurus ... he has made me taste the sweets of innocence, and brought me into the*

calm of philosophy. It is thus, by rendering us happy, that he lays us at his feet.

He cannot but know his power, yet he exerts it in no other way, than to mend our lives, or to keep them innocent.

Candor, as you have already remarked, is prominent feature of his mind, the crown of his perfect character.

Beholding the wisdom and virtue of a sage is crucial. The ultimate authority, however, is always the canon: the natural faculties by which we directly apprehend reality. It is this canon that vindicates a true sage. Once Theon (a Stoic who stumbles into Epicurus and must confront his deep-seated and demoralizing prejudices against hedonist philosophy) has his false notions put in their right place, Epicurus encourages him to think for himself based on the immediacy of his direct experience.

Learn henceforth to form judgements upon knowledge, not report. Credulity is always a ridiculous, often a dangerous failing.

The Abstract Versus the Real

We see an attack on Stoic and Platonic tendencies to speak of abstractions instead of addressing reality as it is, in the following quote attributed to Epicurus in the text.

Zeno hath his eye on man, I mine on men: none but philosophers can be stoics; Epicureans all may be.

Man, as an abstract idea removed from material reality and context, is contrasted here with men as individuals that exist interwoven with reality and context. The effect that this is said to have is that only philosophers can be stoics, but all may be Epicureans. To paraphrase the book, Zeno sees man as he should be; Epicurus sees him as he is. This is an important insight, and one that Thomas Jefferson in his Epistle to Peter Carr elaborated:

He who made us would have been a pitiful bungler, if he had made the rules of our moral conduct a matter of science. For one man of science, there are thousands who are not. What would have become of them?

Man was destined for society. His morality, therefore, was to be formed to this object. He was endowed with a sense of right and wrong, merely relative to this. This sense is as much a part of his Nature, as the sense of hearing, seeing, feeling; it is the true foundation of morality, and not the [beautiful], truth, etc., as fanciful writers have imagined.

The moral sense, or conscience, is as much a part of man as his leg or arm. It is given to all human beings in a stronger or weaker degree, as force of members is given them in a greater or less degree. It may be strengthened by exercise, as may any particular limb of the body. This sense is submitted, indeed, in some degree, to the guidance of reason; but it is a small stock which is required for this: even a less one than what we call common sense. State a moral case to a ploughman and a professor. The former will decide it as well, and often better than the latter, because he has not been led astray by artificial rules.

In a similar vein, later in the text there is a reference to how words are to things what means are to the end. When it is explained that virtue is happiness, it is understood that men speak of virtue (which is the means) as the end (which is really happiness) because they haven't been able to distinguish the abstract conception of the pleasant from the real experience of pleasure.

> *I feel myself virtuous because my soul is at rest. – Epicurus, in A Few Days in Athens*

Virtue and happiness (abiding pleasure) can be said to be one and the same insofar as one is the means to the other.

> *Of all the thousands who have yielded homage to virtue, hardly one has thought of inspecting the pedestal she stands upon.*

Just as good and virtue equals pleasure, similarly evil is the abstraction to refer to pain, which is concrete.

> *With evil passions I should be disturbed and uneasy; with uncontrolled apetites I should be disorded in body as well as mind.*

This important issue of abstractions versus concrete things, and of how words must always have concrete, clear and concise meaning, appears again and again: we find it in Philodemus, and it must be traced back to the original founders of the tradition.

It's even more important when we consider what other philosophers do with rhetoric, how they twist truths and bend them for the benefit of their clients or to demonstrate their ability to persuade, and when we consider the blatant disregard for truth among the rhetors, a matter which will be covered in future reasonings concerning Philodemus' Rhetorica.

Therefore, when discussing philosophy with other schools, as well as with each other, it's important that words are clearly defined in concrete and concise terms to avoid confusion. This subject is revisited later in the text, when Metrodorus critiques the pedantry of Aristotle and how his dark sayings entice the mobs.

The language of truth is too simple for inexperienced ears. We start in search of knowledge like the demi-gods of old in search of adventure, prepared to encounter giants, to scale mountains ... to find none of these

*things, but in their stead, a smooth road
through a pleasant country with a familiar
guide to direct our curiosity and point out
the beauties of the landscape, disappoints us
of all exploit and all notoriety; and our
vanity turns too often from the fair and open
fields into error's dark labyrinths, where we
mistake mystery for wisdom, pedantry for
knowledge, and prejudice for virtue.*

By Their Fruits Ye Shall Know Them

The above quote is associated with Jesus in
the Gospels, but Wright appropriated it and
prophetically placed it on the lips of Epicurus
during a discussion with Zeno on the future
decay and the future reputations of their
respective schools, both of which they
anticipate will be calumniated by "ambitious
bigots".

*From the flavor, we pronounce of the fruit;
from the beauty and the fragrance of the
flower; and in a system of morals, or of
philosophy, or of whatever else, what tends
to produce good we pronounce to be good,
what to produce evil, we pronounce to be
evil.*

We are here invited to judge each philosophy by the good it does (the pleasure it confers) and the evil (suffering) it prevents. If by these simple criteria we were to judge religions and philosophies prominent today, this would help us to judge Islam, Christianity, Marxism and other worldviews in light of historical and contemporary events (including how much violence and suffering they have produced) with a lucid and sober mind. Unlike political correctness, bigotries and bias, the pain and pleasure principle are not subjective or relative. They are real, natural, observable, concrete experiences.

"I gently awaken their sleeping faculties ..."

The above considerations regarding virtue and pleasure, and how (guided by nature) one must distinguish them as the means and the end, have specific repercussions on the way in which Zeno and Epicurus teach philosophy.

Epicurus concedes that Stoics are virtuous as well, but the severity and gravity of Zeno is contrasted beautifully against the compassion and the sweet mellows Epicurean philosophy.

With all his weaknesses, all his errors, all his sins ... I call from my Gardens to the thoughtless, the headstrong, and the idle. "Where do ye wander, and what do ye seek? Is it pleasure? Behold it here. Is it ease? Enter and repose." Thus do I court them from the table of drunkenness and the bed of licentiousness: I gently awaken their sleeping faculties, and draw the veil from their understandings.

"My sons, do you seek pleasure? I seek her also. Let us make the search together. You have tried wine, you have tried love; you have sought amusement in revelling, and forgetfulness in indolence. You tell me you are disappointed: that your passions grew, even while you gratified them; your weariness increased even while you slept. Let us try again. Let us quiet our passions, not by gratifying but subduing them; let us conquer our weariness, not by rest, but by exertion."

Thus do I win their ears and their confidence. Step by step I lead them on ...

Temperance presides at the repast; innocence, at the festival; disgust is changed

> *to satisfaction; listlessness, to curiosity;*
> *brutality, to elegance; lust gives place to*
> *love; Bacchanalian hilarity to friendship.*

The contrast here lies in Epicurean insistence of gently yielding to the good in our nature, rather than the authoritarian, repressive approach of the Stoics. This is consistent with the proper understanding of virtue as not arising from some arbitrary or authoritarian principle (such as duty) but rather as that which gives way to the most pleasant existence. Let's call this
the grassroots understanding of virtue, since it is not implemented from the top-down, but organically.

Part of how Epicurus plants the seeds of his Garden and of pleasure and virtue in the hearts of his followers is by inflaming them with love of wisdom and of philosophy, and with a sense of fraternity with each other. A Few Days in Athens describes the serene life of philosophy in the most sublime manner.

> *A happy life is like neither to a roaring*
> *torrent, nor a stagnant pool, but to a placid*
> *and crystal stream that flows gently and*

silently along.

The text goes on to list all the virtues and how they make life pleasant, and insightfully ends up recognizing the relationship that philosophy has to nature.

True, Philosophy cannot change the laws of nature; but she may teach us to accomodate to them. She cannot annul pain; but she can arm us to bear it.

This passage begins a wonderful litany in praise of philosophy and what she can do for our souls, and concludes:

This ... is our interest and our hapiness: to seek our pleasures from the hands of the virtues, and for the pain which may befall us, to submit to it with patience, or bear up against it with fortutide. To walk ... through life innocently and tranquilly: and to look on death as its gentle termination, which it becomes us to meet with ready minds, neither regretting the past, nor anxious for the future.

A Mind Free of Prejudice

The final portion of the book is perhaps the most controversial and difficult part, as it contains a polemic against conventional beliefs about God and a defense of atheism. It calls for questioning religious beliefs and a blissful indifference to deity. This is the part of the book that is most reminiscent to contemporary militant atheist authors, except that here the polemic is contextualized within Epicurean discourse and it does not specifically constitute a call to atheism as much as a call to end prejudice against atheists and against atheism.

Wright's Epicurus had to first break the ice and challenge Theon's blind adherence to Stoic doctrines about the Gods. He begins by challenging how a belief can be considered a crime or a virtue, as this attaches merit to credulity, and furthermore attaches demerit to investigation.

If the doubt of any truth shall constitute a crime, then the belief of the same truth should constitute a virtue.

The conversation then focuses on whether the mind has the power to believe or disbelieve, at pleasure, any truths whatsoever, or whether it possesses the power of investigation. In other words, do we owe it to ourselves to investigate truth claims? Do we even hold truth in high regard? Do we arrogantly believe as we wish, regardless of facts, or of the cost to our safety or to our lives of the tenets we hold?

A prudent and fair person can here only agree that investigation is necessary and a matter of intellectual decency. Therefore, it is fair to investigate whether the Gods exist or not, and it is fair to refrain from reaching a conclusion until we can directly apprehend them. Doubt is not a crime and unjustified certainty is not a virtue.

You enquire if the doctrine we have essayed to establish, be not dangerous. I reply, not if it be true. Nothing is so dangerous as error, nothing so safe as truth.

When asked by Theon what is truth and what

is the fixed basis for it, Wright's Epicurus answers:

> *A truth I consider to be an ascertained fact; which truth would be changed into an error, the moment the fact on which it rested was disproved. (Truth) surely has the most fixed (basis) of all: the nature of things, and it is only an imperfect insight into that nature which occasions all our erroneous conclusions, whether in physics or morals.*

This notion of how one truth leads to another truth in a chain of causation is then elaborated into a sermon on the importance of attaching ourselves to empirical evidence and to our senses and faculties, since if the senses are denied, we are "set on wrong path as false views lead to more false views".

The point of the anti-theological sermon is that we must free our minds from prejudice and from cultural corruption. Unlike religion and cultural values, science and empirical accumulation of knowledge are free from bias.

Chapter XIV closes with the following conclusion concerning the supposed immorality of atheism, which was believed by Theon originally to be a thought-crime. After explaining that it is no crime to believe with certainty in gods, but that's it's unreasonnable, Wright's Epicurus closes:

> (Let) this truth remain with you: that an opinion, right or wrong, can never constitute a moral offence, nor be in itself a moral obligation. It may be mistaken; it may involve an absurdity, or a contradiction. It is a truth, or it is an error: it can never be a crime or a virtue.

Leontium then assumes the role of instructor and criticizes Plato's ideas and how theologians and Platonists establish laws and doctrines with no input from the study of nature, leading people into error, upon which of course further error is built.

> A theory is built, and all animate and inanimate nature is made to speak in its support; an hypothesis is advanced and all the mysteries of nature are treated as explained.

Here, she would be making a mockery of

Mormon "archaeogists" who have journeyed in vain to the lands of the first nations in the Americas in search of proof of the people and places of the mythical Book of Mormon, just as many Christians "archaeologists" have done in the Middle East. In this manner, a mind filled with cultural corruption and prejudice will start off on false premises that are unproven, and make the findings and the evidence accomodate to their pre-established views without considering the possibility that they're based on a fraudulent foundation.

> *The science of philosophy is simply a science of observation, both as regards the world without us, and the world within; and to advance in it, are requisite only sound senses, well developed and exercised faculties, and a mind free of prejudice.*

In a later chapter, we find a related sermon against what we might call the god of the gaps: the filling in the spaces of our ignorance with supernatural claims, which are considered evil insofar as they are fear-based and disturb our souls with fears of hell, of death, or of wrathful and tyrannical deities, robbing us of our freedom and happiness. The questions about gods and their nature must be addressed, for they

> *either open our minds to knowledge of the wonders working in and around us, as our senses and faculties can attain, or close them forever with the bands of superstitions, leaving us a prey to fear, the slaves of our ungoverned imagination, wondering and trambling at every occurrence in nature, and making our existence and destiny sources of dread and mystery.*

> *... It behooves us to see that we come with willing minds; that we say not "so far will we go and no farther; we will examine, but only so long as the result of our examination shall confirm our preconceived opinions."*

The First Cause

The didactic novel continues with Theon arguing the existence of God by citing a first cause. It is here that we find the same answer to that argument that has been used by the likes of Richard Dawkins, who asks what caused the first cause: if all things have a cause, we end up right where we started. This is an old argument.

Epicureans have always held that it has never been in evidence that something comes from nothing. All things, when they decompose, their atoms return to the elements and form new things so that although constant change is everywhere in evidence, nothing comes from nothing. The constituents of all things (the atoms) are therefore held to be eternal.

Metrodorus Calls for a Neuroscience

There is no mystery in nature ... things being as they are, is no more wonderful, than it would be if they were different.

Another area where thinkers, both religious and philosophical, have frequently made spurrious claims is the nature of the mind and of consciousness. Wright's Metrodorus bursts the bubble of mystery and awe that surrounds the human mind by proposing a materialist view and explaining that mind is a property of the living and has no existence independent of matter.

No real advances can be made in the philosophy of the mind, without a deep scrutiny into the operations of nature, or material existences. Mind being only a quality of matter, the study we call the philosophy of mind is necessarily only a branch of general physics (the study of nature).

Against Fear-Based Religion

The final portion constitutes a diatribe against religion. The argument that it's useful and that we should consider its utilitarian benefits is refuted with the argument that the world is full of religion and full of misery and crime. The text then goes into a litany of reasons why religion is mischievous and laments the state of the men who practice fear-based religion.

His best faculties dormant; his judgment unawakened; his very senses misemployed; all his energies misdirected; trembling before the coinage of his own idle fancy; seeing over all creation a hand of tyranny extended; and instead of following virtue, worshipping power! Monstrous creation of Ignorance! … Man, boasting of superior reason, of moral discrimination, imagines a being at once unjust, cruel, and inconsistent, then kissing the dust, calls himself its slave.

> *To fear a being on account of his power is degrading, to fear him as he be good, ridiculous.*

It is here that we find a detailed elaboration of Epicurus' Trilemma, which says:

> *(1) If God is unable to prevent evil, he is not omnipotent.*
> *(2) If God is not willing to prevent evil, he is not good.*
> *(3) If God is willing and able to prevent evil, then why is there evil?*
> *— Epicurus Trilemma*

The theologian is then invited to banish fear and doubt from his creed, for love alone can be claimed by gods or yielded by men. The problem of fear-based religion and of the vulgar notions that people have about wrathful gods who interfere in human affairs is tackled one last time on the grounds of how degrading these beliefs are to humans.

> *Theist! You make your god a being more weak, more silly than yourself.*

The final portion closes with the argument

that if a God exists, any being worthy of the name God would want us to be happy and would be concerned with its own happiness and pleasure, wishing us to focus on our own. Therefore, the conclusion of all these reasonings is that we should:

Enjoy, and be happy! Do you doubt the way? Let Epicurus be your guide. The source of every enjoyment is within yourselves. Good and evil lie before you. the good is all which can yield you pleasure; the evil, what must bring you pain. Here is no paradox, no dark saying, no moral hid in fables.

A FEW DAYS IN ATHENS

Being
THE TRANSLATION Of A GREEK MANUSCRIPT
Discovered In Herculaneum
BY FRANCES WRIGHT
Author of *"Views of Society And Manners In America"*

"– joining bliss to virtue the glad ease
Of Epicurus, seldom understood."
– Thomson's *Liberty*

Dedication

TO JEREMY BENTHAM,
AS A TESTIMONY OF HER ADMIRATION OF HIS
ENLIGHTENED SENTIMENTS, USEFUL LABOURS,
AND ACTIVE PHILANTHROPY, AND OF HER
GRATITUDE FOR HIS FRIENDSHIP, THIS WORK IS
RESPECTFULLY AND AFFECTIONATELY
INSCRIBED, BY

FRANCES WRIGHT

London,
March 12th, 1822.

Chapter 1

"Oh monstrous," cried the young Theon, as he came from the portico of Zeno. "Ye Gods! and will ye suffer your names to be thus blasphemed? How do ye not strike with thunder the actor and teacher of such enormities? What! will ye suffer our youth, and the youth of after ages, to be seduced by this shameless Gargettian? Shall the Stoic portico be forsaken for the garden of Epicurus? Minerva, shield thy city! XXX Shut the ears of thy sons against the voice of this deceiver!"

Thus did Theon give vent to the indignation which the words of Timocrates had worked up within him. Timocrates had been a disciple of the new school; but, quarreling with his master, had fled to the followers of Zeno; and to make the greater merit of his apostacy, and better to gain the hearts of his new friends, poured forth daily execrations on his former teacher, painting him and his disciples in the blackest colours of deformity; revealing, with a countenance distorted as with horror, and a voice hurried and suppressed as from the agonies of dreadful recollections, the secrets of those midnight orgies, where, in the midst of his pupils, the philosopher of Gargettium officiated as master of the cursed ceremonies of riot and impiety.

Full of these nocturnal horrors, the young Theon traversed with hasty steps the streets of Athens, and issuing from the city, without perceiving that he did so, took the road to the Piraeus. The noise of the harbor roused him to recollection, and, feeling it out of tune with his thoughts, he turned up the more peaceful banks of the Cephisus, and, seating himself on the stump of a withered olive, his feet almost washed by the water, he fell back again into his reverie. How long he had sat he knew not, when the sound of gently approaching footsteps once more recalled him. He turned his head, and, after a start and gaze of astonishment, bent with veneration to the figure before him. It was of the middle size, and robed in white, pure as the vestments of the Pythia. The shape, the attitude, the foldings of the garment, were such as the chisel of Phidias would have given to the God of Elocution. The head accorded with the rest of the figure; it sat upon the shoulders with a grace that a painter would have paused to contemplate — elevated, yet somewhat inclining forward, as if habituated gently to seek and benevolently to yield attention. The face a poet would have gazed upon, and thought he beheld in it one of the images of his fancy embodied. The features were not cast for the statuary; they were noble, but not regular. Wisdom beamed mildly from the eye, and candor was on the broad forehead, the mouth reposed in a soft, almost imperceptible smile, that did not curl the lips or disturb the cheeks, and was seen only in the serene and holy benignity that shone over the whole physiognomy: it was a gleam of sunshine sleeping on a lucid lake. The first lines of age were traced on the brow and round the chin, but so gently as to mellow rather than deepen expression: the hair indeed seemed prematurely touched by time, for it was of a pure silver, thrown back from the forehead, and fringing the throat behind with short curls. He received benignly the salutation of the youth, and gently with his hand returning it — "Let me not break your meditations; I would rather share than disturb them." If the stranger's appearance had enchanted Theon, his voice did now more so; never had a sound so sweet, so musical, struck upon his ear.

"Surely I behold and hear a divinity," he cried, stepping backwards, and half-stooping his knee with veneration.

"From the groves of the Academy, I see," said the sage, advancing, and laying his hand on the youth's shoulder.

Theon looked up with a modest blush, and, encouraged by the sweet aspect of the sage, replied, "No; from the portico."

"Ah! I had not thought Zeno could send forth such a dreamer. You are in a good school," he continued, observing the youth confused by his remark, "a school of real virtue; and, if I read faces well, as I think I do, I see a pupil that will not disgrace its doctrines."

Theon's spirit returned; the stranger had that look, and voice, and manner, which instantly give security to the timid, and draw love from the feeling heart. "If you be man, you exert more than human influence over the souls of your fellows. I have seen you but one moment, and that moment has laid me at your feet."

"Not quite so low, I hope," returned the sage,

with a smile; "I had always rather be the companion than the master."

"Either, both," said the eager youth, and, seizing the half-extended hand of the sage, pressed it respectfully to his lips.

"You are an enthusiast, I see. Beware, my young friend! Such as you must be the best or the worst of men."

"Then, had I you for a guide, I should be the best."

"What! do you, a stoic, ask a guide?"

"I, a stoic! Oh, would I were; I yet stand but on the threshold of the temple."

"But, standing there, you have at least looked within and seen the glories, and will not that encourage you to advance? Who that hath seen virtue doth not love her, and pant after her possession?"

"True, true; I have seen virtue in her noblest form—alas! so noble, that my eyes have been dazzled by the contemplation. I have looked upon Zeno with admiration and despair."

"Learn rather to look with love. He who but admires virtue, yields her but half her due. She asks to be approached, to be embraced — not with fear, but with confidence — not with awe, but with rapture."

"Yet who can gaze on Zeno, and ever hope to rival him?"

"You, my young friend: Why should you not? You have innocence; you have sensibility; you have enthusiasm; you have ambition. With what better promise could Zeno begin his career. Courage! courage! my son! stopping, for they had insensibly walked towards the city during the dialogue, and laying his hand on Theon's head, "we want but the will to be as great as Zeno."

Theon had drawn his breath for a sigh, but this action and the look that accompanied it, changed the sigh to a smile. "You would make me vain."

"No; but I would make you confident. Without confidence Homer had never written his Iliad. No, nor would Zeno now be worshiped in his portico."

"Do you then think confidence would make all men Homers and Zenos!"

"Not all; but a good many. I believe thousands to have the seeds of excellence in them, who never discover the possession. But we were not speaking of poetry and philosophy, only of virtue — all men certainly cannot be poets or philosophers, but all men may be virtuous."

"I believe," returned the youth with a modest blush, "if I might walk with you each day on the borders of Cephisus, I should sometimes play truant at the portico."

"Ye gods forbid," exclaimed the sage, playfully, "that I should steal a proselyte! From Zeno, too? It might cost me dear. — What are you thinking of?" he resumed, after a pause.

"I was thinking," replied Theon, "what a loss for man that you are not teacher in the gardens in place of the son of Neocles."

"The gods forbid that I should know him more than by report! No, venerable stranger; wrong me not so much as to think I have entered the gardens of Epicurus. It is not long that I have been in Athens, but I hope, if I should henceforth live my life here, I shall never be seduced by the advocate of vice."

"From my soul I hope the same. But you say you have not long been in Athens. You are come here to study philosophy."

"Yes; my father was a scholar of Xenocrates; but when he sent me from Corinth, he bade me attend all the schools, and fix with that which should give me the highest views of virtue."

"And you have found it to be that of Zeno."

"I think I have: but I was one day nearly gained by a young Pythagorean, and have been often in danger of becoming one of the academy."

You need not say *in danger*: for, though I think

you choose well in standing mainly by Zeno, I would have you attend all the schools, and that with a willing ear. There is some risk in following one particular sect, even the most perfect, lest the mind become warped and the heart contracted. Yes, young man! it is possible that this should happen even in the portico. No sect without its prejudices and its predilections."

"I believe you say true."

"I *know* I say true," returned the sage, in a tone of playfulness he had more than once used; I *know* I say true; and had I before needed evidence to confirm my opinion, this our present conversation would have afforded it."

"How so!"

"Nay, were I to explain, you would not now credit me; no man can see his own prejudices; no, though a philosopher should point at them. But patience, patience! Time and opportunity shall right all things. Why, you did not think," he resumed, after a short pause, "you did not really think you were without prejudices? Eighteen, not more, if I may judge by complexion, and without prejudices! Why, I should hardly dare to assert I was myself without them, and I believe I have fought harder and somewhat longer against them than you can have done."

"What would you have me do!" asked the youth timidly.

"Have you do? Why, I would have you do a very odd thing. No other than to take a turn or two in Epicurus' garden."

"Epicurus' garden! Oh, Jupiter!"

"Very true, by Juno."

"What! To hear the laws of virtue confounded and denied? To hear vice exculpated, advocated, panegyrised? Impiety and atheism professed and inculcated? To witness the nocturnal orgies of vice and debauchery? Ye gods, what horrors has Timocrates revealed!"

"Horrors, in truth, somewhat appalling, my young friend; but I should apprehend Timocrates to be a little mistaken. That the laws of virtue were ever confounded and denied, or vice advocated and panegyrised, by any professed teacher, I incline to doubt. And were I really to hear such things, I should simply conclude the speaker mad, or otherwise that he was amusing himself by shifting the meaning of words, and that by the term virtue, he understood vice, and so by the contrary. As to the inculcating of impiety and atheism, this may be exaggerated or misunderstood. Many are called impious not for having a worse, but a different religion from their neighbors ; and many atheistical, not for the denying of God, but for thinking somewhat peculiarly concerning him. Upon the nocturnal orgies of vice and debauchery I can say nothing; I am too profoundly ignorant of these matters either to exculpate or condemn them. Such things may be, and I never hear of them. All things are possible. Yes," turning his benignant face full upon the youth, "even that Timocrates should lie."

"This possibility had indeed not occurred to me."

"No, my young friend; and shall I tell you why? Because he told you absurdities. Let an impostor keep to probability, and he will hardly impose. By dealing in the marvelous, he tickles the imagination, and carries away the judgment; and, judgment once gone, what shall save even a wise man from folly?"

"I should truly rejoice to find the Gargettian's doctrines less monstrous than I have hitherto thought them. I say *less monstrous*, for you would not wish me to think them good."

"I would wish you to think nothing good, or bad either, upon my decision. The first and the last thing I would say to man is, *think for yourself.* It is a bad sentence of the Pythagoreans, 'The master said so.' If the young disciple you mentioned should ever succeed in your conversion, believe in the metempsychosis for some other reason than that Pythagoras 'taught it.'"

"But if I may ask, do you think well of Epicurus?"

"I meant not to make an apology for Epicurus, only to give a caution against Timocrates — but see, we are in the city; and, fortunately so, for it is pretty nigh dark. I have a party of young friends awaiting me, and, but that you may be apprehensive of nocturnal orgies, I would ask you to join us."

"I shall not fear them where I have such a conductor," replied the youth, laughing.

"I do not think it quite so impossible, however, as you seem to do," said the sage, laughing, in his turn, with much humor, and entering a house as he spoke; then throwing open with one arm a door, and with the other gently drawing the youth along with him, "I am Epicurus."

CHAPTER II.

The astonished, the affrighted Theon, started from the arm of the sage, and, staggering backwards, was saved, probably from falling, by a statue that stood against the wall on one side of the door; he leaned against it, pale and almost fainting. He knew not what to do, scarcely what to feel, and was totally blind to all the objects around him. His conductor, who had possibly expected his confusion, did not turn to observe it, but advanced in such a manner as to cover him from the view of the company, and, still to give time for recollection, stood receiving and returning salutations.

"Well met, my sons! and I suppose you say well met, also. Are you starving, or am I to be starved? Have you eat up the supper, or only sat longing for it, cursing my delay?"

"The latter, only the latter," cried a lively youth, hurrying to meet his master. Another and another advanced, and in a moment he was locked in a close circle.

"Mercy! mercy!" cried the philosopher, "drive

me a step further, and you will overturn a couple of statues." Then, looking over his shoulder, I have brought you, if he has not run away, a very pleasant young Corinthian, for whom, until he gain his own tongue, I shall demand reception." He held out his hand with a look of bewitching encouragement, and the yet faltering Theon advanced. The mist had now passed from his eyes, and the singing from his ears, and both room and company stood revealed before him. Perhaps, had it not been for this motion, and still more this look of the sage, he had just now made a retreat instead of an advance." In the hall of Epicurus — in that hall where Timocrates had beheld" oh, horrid imagination! "And he a disciple of Zeno, the friend of Cleanthes — the son of a follower of Plato — had he crossed the threshold of vice, the threshold of the impious Gargettian;" Yes; he had certainly fled, but for that extended hand, and that bewitching smile. These however conquered. He advanced, and, with an effort at composure, met the offered hand. The circle made way, and Epicurus presented 'a friend.' "His name you must learn from himself, I am only acquainted with his heart, and that on a knowledge of two hours, I pronounce myself in love with."

"Then he shall be my brother," cried the lively youth who had before spoken, and he ran to the embrace of Theon.

"When shall we use our own eyes, ears, and understandings" said the sage, gently stroking his scholar's head. " See our new friend knows not how to meet your premature affection."

"He waits," returned the youth archly, "to receive the same commendation of me that I have of him. Let the master say he is in love with my heart, and he too will open his arms to a brother."

"I hope he is not such a fool," gaily replied the sage. Then, with an accent more serious, but still sweeter, " I hope he will judge all things, and all people, with his own understanding, and not with that of Epicurus, or yet of a wiser man. "When may I hope this of Sofron?" smiling and shaking his head; "can Sofron tell me?"

"No, indeed he cannot," rejoined the scholar, smiling and shaking his head also, as in mimicry of his master.

"Go, go, you rogue! and show us to our supper: I more than half suspect you have devoured it." He turned, and' familiarly taking Theon by the shoulder, walked up the room, or rather gallery, and entered a spacious rotunda.

A lamp, suspended from the centre of the ceiling, lighted a table spread beneath it, with, a simple but elegant repast. Round the walls, in niches at equal distances, stood twelve statues, the work of the best masters; on either hand of these burnt a lamp on a small tripod. Beside one of the lamps, a female figure was reclining on a couch, reading with earnest study from a book that lay upon her knee. Her head was so much bowed forward as to conceal her face, besides that it was shadowed by her hand, which, the elbow supported on an arm of the couch, was spread above her brows as a relief from the glare of the light. At her feet was seated a young girl by whose side lay a small cithara, silent and forgotten by its mistress. Crete might have lent those eyes their sparkling jet, but all the soul of tenderness that breathed from them was pure

Ionian. The full and ruddy lips, half parted, showed two rows of pearls, which Thetis might have envied. Still a vulgar eye would not have rested on the countenance: the features wanted the Doric harmony, and the complexion was tinged as by an Afric sun. Theon, however, saw not this, as his eyes fell on those of the girl, uplifted to the countenance of her studious companion. Never was a book read more earnestly than was that face by the fond and gentle eyes which seemed to worship as they gazed. The sound of approaching feet caught the ear of the maiden. She rose, blushed, half returned the salute of the master, and timidly drew back some paces. The student was still intent upon the scroll over which she hung, when the sage advanced towards her and laying a finger on her shoulder, "What read you my daughter?" She dropt her hand, and looked up in his face. What a countenance was then revealed! It was not the beauty of blooming, blushing youth, courting love and desire. It was the self-possessed dignity of ripened womanhood, and the noble majesty of mind, that asked respect and promised delight and instruction. The features were not those of Venus, but Minerva. The eyes looked deep and steady from beneath two even brows, that sense, not years, had slightly knit in centre of the forehead, which else was uniformly smooth, and polished as marble. The nose was rather Roman than Grecian, yet perfectly regular, and, though not masculine, would have been severe in expression, but for a mouth where all that was lovely and graceful habited. The chin was elegantly rounded, and turned in the Greek manner. The colour of the cheeks was of the softest and palest rose, so pale, indeed, as scarcely to be discernible until deepened by emotion. It was so at this moment: startled by the address of the sage, a bright flush passed over her face. She rolled up the book, dropped it on the couch, and rose. Her stature was much above the female standard, but every limb and every motion was symmetry and harmony. "A treatise of Theophrastus; — eloquent, ingenious, and chimerical. I have a fancy to answer it." Her voice was lull and deep, like the tones of a harp, when its chords are struck by the hands of a master.

"No one could do it better," replied the sage. But I should have guessed the aged Peripatetic already silenced by the most acute, elegant, and subtle pen of Athens." She bowed to the compliment.

"Is that then the famous Leontium?" muttered Theon. "Timocrates must be a liar."

"I know not," resumed Leontium, "that I should this evening have so frequently thought Theophrastus wrong, if he had not made me so continually feel that he thought himself right. Must I seek the cause of this in the writer's or the reader's vanity?"

"Perhaps," said the master, smiling, " you will find that it lies in both."

"I believe you have it," returned Leontium. "Theophrastus, in betraying his self-love, hurt mine. He who is about to prove that his own way of thinking is right, must bear in mind, that he is about also to prove that all other ways of thinking are wrong. And if this should make him slow to enter on the undertaking, it should make him yet more careful, when he does enter on it, to do it with becoming modesty. We are surely imperiously called upon to make a sacrifice of our own vanity, before we call upon others to make a sacrifice of theirs. But I would not particularize Theophrastus for sometimes forgetting this, as I have never known but one who always remembers it. Gentleness and modesty are qualities at once the most indispensable to a teacher, and the most rarely possessed by him. It was these that won the ears of the Athenian youth to Socrates, and it is these," inclining to the master, "that will secure them to Epicurus."

"Could I accept your praise, my daughter, I should have no doubt of the truth of your prophecy. For, indeed, the mode of delivering a truth makes, for the most part, as much impression on the mind of the listener, as the truth itself. It is as hard to receive the words of wisdom from the ungentle, as it is to love, or even to recognize virtue in the austere." He drew near the table as he spoke. Often during supper were the eyes of Theon riveted on the face of this female disciple. Such grace! such majesty! More than all such intellect! And this — this was the Leontium Timocrates had called a prostitute without shame or measure! And this was the Epicurus he had blasted with names too vile and horrible to repeat even in thought! And these

— continuing his inward soliloquy as he looked round the board — these were the devoted victims of the vice of an impious master.

"You arrived most seasonably this evening," cried Sofron, addressing the philosopher; "most seasonably for the lungs of two of your scholars."

"And for the ears of a third," interrupted Leontium. "I was fairly driven into exile."

"What was the subject?" asked Epicurus.

"Whether the vicious were more justly objects of indignation or of contempt: Metrodorus argued for the first, and I for the latter. Let the master decide."
"He will give his opinion certainly; but that is not decision."

"Well: and your opinion is that of ----."

"Neither."

"Neither! I had no idea the question had more than two sides."

"It has yet a third; and I hardly ever heard a question that had not. Had I regarded the vicious with indignation, I had never gained one to virtue. Had I viewed them with contempt, I had never sought to gain one."

"How is it," said Leontium, "that the scholars are so little familiar with the temper of their master? When did Epicurus look on the vicious with other than compassion?"

"True," said Metrodorus. "I know not how I forgot this, when perhaps it is the only point which I have, more than once, presumed to argue with him; and upon which I have persisted in retaining a different opinion."

"Talk not of presumption, my son. Who has not a right to think for himself? Or, who is he whose voice is infallible, and worthy to silence those of his fellow men? And remember, that your remaining unconvinced by my argument on one occasion, can only tend to make your conviction more flattering to me upon others. Yet, on the point in question, were I anxious to bring you over to my opinion I know one, whose argument, better and more forcible than mine, will ere long most effectually do so."

"Who mean you ?"

"No other than old hoary Time," said the master, "who, as he leads us gently onwards in the path of life, demonstrates to us many truths that we never heard in the schools, and some that, hearing there, we found hard to receive. Our knowledge of human life must be acquired by our passage through it; the lessons of the sage are not sufficient to impart it. Our knowledge of men must be acquired by our own study of them; the report of others will never convince us. When you, my son, have seen more of life, and studied more men, you will find, or, at least, I *think* you will find, that the judgment is not false which makes us lenient to the failings — yea! even to the crimes of our fellows. In youth, we act on the impulse of feeling, and we feel without pausing to judge. An action, vicious in itself, or that is so merely in our estimation, fills us with horror, and we turn from its agent without waiting to listen to the plea which his ignorance could make to our mercy. In our ripened years, supposing our judgment to have ripened also, when all the insidious temptations that misguided him, and all the disadvantages that he has labored under, perhaps-from his birth, are apparent to us — it is then, and not till then, that our indignation at the crime is lost in our pity of the man."

"I am the last," said Metrodorus, a crimson blush spreading over his face, "who should object to my master his clemency towards the offending. But there are vices, different from those he saved me from, which, if not more unworthy, are perhaps more unpardonable, because committed with less temptation; and more revolting, as springing less from thoughtless ignorance than calculating depravity."

"Are we not prone," said the sage, "to extenuate our foibles, even while condemning them? And does it not flatter our self-love, to weigh our own vices against those of more erring neighbors?"

The scholar leaned forwards, and stooping his face towards the hand of his master, where it rested on the table, laid the deepening crimsons of his cheek upon it. "I mean not to exculpate the early vices of Metrodorus. I love to consider them in all their enormity; for the more heinous the vices of his youth, the greater is the debt of gratitude his manhood has to repay to thee. But tell me," he added, and lifted his eyes to the benignant face of the sage, "tell me, oh, my friend and guide! was the soul of Metrodorus found base or deceitful; or has his heart proved false to gratitude and affection?"

"No, my son, no," said Epicurus, his face beaming with goodness, and a tear glistening in his eye. "No! Vice never choked the warm feelings of thy heart, nor clouded the fair ingenuousness of thy soul. But, my son, a few years later — a few years later, and who shall say what *might* have been! Trust me, none can drink of the cup of vice with impunity." But you will say, that there are qualities of so mean or so horrible a nature, as to place the man that is governed by them out of the pale of communion with the virtuous. Malice, cruelty, deceit, ingratitude — crimes such as these, should, you think, draw down upon those convicted of them, no feelings more mild than abhorrence, execration, and scorn.

And yet, perhaps, these were not always natural to the heart they now sway. Fatal impressions, vicious example, operating on the plastic frame of childhood, may have perverted all the fair gifts of nature, may have distorted the tender plant from the seedling, and crushed all the blossoms of virtue in the germ. Say, shall we not compassionate the moral disease of our brother, and try our skill to restore him to health? But is the evil beyond cure? Is the mind strained into changeless deformity, and the heart corrupted in the core? Greater, then, much greater will be our compassion. For is not his wretchedness complete, when his errors are without hope of correction? Oh, my sons! the wicked may work mischief to others, but they never can inflict a pang such as they endure themselves. I am satisfied, that of all the miseries that tear the heart of man, none may compare with those it feels beneath the sway of baleful passions."

"Oh," cried Theon, turning with a timid blush towards Epicurus, "I have long owned the power of virtue, but surely till this night I never felt its persuasion."
"I see you were not born for a stoic," said the

master, smiling, "Why, my son, what made you fall in love with Zeno?"

"His virtues," said the youth, proudly.

"His fine face and fine talking," returned the philosopher, with a tone of playful irony. "Nay! don't be offended;" and he stretched his hand to Theon's shoulder, who reclined on the sofa next him. "I admire your master very much, and go to hear him very often."

"Indeed!"

"Indeed? Yes, indeed. Is it so wonderful?"

"You were not there." — Theon stopped and looked down in confusion.

"To-day, you mean? Yes, I was; and heard a description of myself that might match in pleasantry with that in 'The Clouds' of old Socrates. Pray don't you find it very like?" He leaned over the side of the couch, and looked in Theon's face.

"I — I" — The youth stammered and looked down. "Think it is," said the sage, as if concluding the sentence for him.

"No, think it is not; swear it is not," burst forth the eager youth, and looked as he would have thrown himself at the philosopher's feet. "Oh! why did you not stand forth and silence the liar?"

"Truly, my son, the liar was too pleasant to be angry with, and too absurd to be answered."

"And yet he was believed?"

"Of course."

"But why then not answer him?"

"And so I do. I answer him in my life. The only way in which a philosopher should ever answer a fool, or, as in this case, a knave."

"I am really bewildered," cried Theon, gazing in the philosopher's and then in Leontium's countenance, and then throwing a glance round the circle. "I am really bewildered with astonishment and shame," he continued, casting down his eyes, "that I should have listened to that liar Timocrates! What a fool you must think me!"

"No more of a fool than Zeno," said the sage, laughing, "What a philosopher listened to, I cannot much blame a scholar for believing."

"Oh, that Zeno knew you!"

"And then he would certainly hate me."

"You joke."

"Quite serious. Don't you know that who quarrels with your doctrine, must always quarrel with your practice? Nothing is so provoking as that a man should preach viciously and act virtuously."

"But you do not preach viciously."

"I hope not. But those will call it so, aye! and in honest heart think it so, who preach a different, it need not be a *better*, doctrine."

"But Zeno mistakes your doctrine."

"I have no doubt he expounds it wrong."
"He mistakes it altogether. He believes that

you own no other law — no other principle of action — than pleasure."
"He believes right."

"Right? Impossible! That you teach men to laugh at virtue, and to riot in luxury and vice."

"There he believes wrong."

Theon looked as he felt, curious and uncertain. He gazed first on the philosopher, and, when he did not proceed, timidly round the circle. Every face had a smile on it.

"The orgies are concluded," said Epicurus, rising, and turning with affected gravity to the young Corinthian. "You have seen the horrors of the night; if they have left any curiosity for the mysteries of the day, seek our garden to-morrow at sun-rise, and you shall be initiated."

CHAPTER III.

The steeds of the sun had not mounted the horizon when Theon took the road to the gardens. He found the gate open. The path he entered on was broad and even, and shaded on either side by rows of cork, lime, oak, and other the finest trees of the forest: pursuing this for some way, he suddenly opened on a fair and varied lawn, through which the Illissus, now of the whitest silver in the pale twilight, stole with a gentle and noiseless course. Crossing the lawn, he struck into a close thicket: the orange, the laurel, and the myrtle, hung over his head, whose flowers, slowly opening to the breeze and light of morning, dropped dews and perfumes. A luxurious indolence crept over his soul; he breathed the airs, and felt the bliss of Elysium. With slow and measured steps he threaded the maze, till he entered suddenly on a small open plot of verdure, in face of a beautiful temple. The place was three parts encircled with a wood of flowering shrubs, the rest was girded by the winding Illissus, over which the eye wandered to glades and softly swelling hills, whose bosoms now glowed beneath the dyes of Aurora. The building was small and circular; Doric, and of the marble of Paros: an open portico, supported by twenty pillars, ran round the edifice: the roof rose in a dome. The roseate tints of the east fell on the polished columns, like the blush of love on the cheek of Diana, when, she stood before her Endymion.

Theon stopped: the scene was heavenly. Long had he gazed in silent and calm delight, when his eye was attracted by the waving of a garment on one side of the temple. He advanced, and beheld a figure leaning against one of the pillars. The sun at that moment shot his first beam above the hills: it fell full upon the face of the son of Neocles: it was raised, and the eyes were fixed as in deep meditation. The features reposed in the calm of wisdom: the arms were folded, and the drapery fell in masses to the feet. Theon flew towards him, then suddenly stopped, fearing to break upon his thoughts. At the sound, the sage turned his head — "Welcome, my son," he said, advancing to meet him, "welcome to the gardens of pleasure; may you find it the abode of peace, of wisdom, and of virtue."

Theon bowed his head upon the hand of the

master. "Teach me, guide me, make me what you will — my soul is in your hand."

"It is yet tender, yet pure," said the Gargettian; "years shall strengthen it. Oh! let them not sully it! See to that luminary! lovely and glorious in the dawn, he gathers strength and beauty to his meridian, and passes in peace and grandeur to his rest. So do thou, my son. Open your ears and your eyes; know, and choose what is good; enter the path of virtue, and thou shalt follow it, for you shall find it sweet. Thorns are not in it, nor is it difficult or steep: like the garden you have now entered, all there is pleasure and repose."

"Ah!" cried Theon, "how different is virtue in your mouth and in Zeno's."

"The doctrine of Zeno," replied the sage, "is sublime: many great men shall come from his school; an amiable world, from mine. Zeno has his eye on man — I, mine on men: none but philosophers can be stoics; Epicureans all may be."

"But," asked Theon, "is there more than one virtue?"

"No, but men clothe her differently; some in clouds and thunders; some in smiles and pleasures. Doctors, my son, quarrel more about words than things, and more about the means than the end. In the Portico, in the Lyceum, in the Academy, in the school of Pythagoras, in the Tub of Diogenes, the teacher points you to virtue; in the garden he points you to happiness. Now open your eyes, my son, and examine the two Deities. Say, are they not the same? virtue is it not happiness? and is not happiness, virtue?"

"Is this, then, the secret of your doctrine?"

"No other."

"But — but — where then is the dispute? Truly, as you have said, in words, not things."
"Yes, in a great measure, yet not all together: we are all the wooers of virtue, but we are wooers of a different character."

"And may she not then favor one more than another?"

"That is a question," replied the Gargettian, playfully, " that each will answer in his own favor. If you ask me, he continued, – with one of his sweetest tones and smiles, "I shall say, that I feel myself virtuous, because my soul is at rest."

"If this be your criterion, you should with the stoics deny that pain is an evil."

"By no means: so much the contrary, I hold it the greatest of all evils, and the whole aim of my life, and of my philosophy, is to escape from it. To deny that pain is an evil is such another quibble as the Elean's denial of motion: that must exist to man which exists to his senses; and as to existence or non existence abstracted from them, though it may afford an idle argument for an idle hour, it can never enter as a truth, from which to draw conclusions, in the practical lessons of a master. To deny that pain is an evil seems more absurd than to deny its existence, which has also been done, for its existence is only apparent from its effect upon our senses; how then shall we admit the existence, and deny the effect, which alone forces that admittance? But we will leave these matters to the dialecticians of the Portico. I feel myself virtuous because my soul is at rest. With evil passions I should be disturbed and uneasy; with uncontrolled appetites I should be disordered in body as well as mind — for this reason, and for this reason only, I avoid both."

"Only!"

"Only: virtue is pleasure; were it not so, I should not follow it."

Theon was about to break forth in indignant astonishment: the sage softly laid a hand upon his arm, and, with a smile and bend of the head demanding attention, proceeded; "The masters who would have us to follow virtue for her own sake, independent of any pleasure or advantage that we may find in the pursuit, are sublime visionaries, who build a theory without examining the ground on which they build it, who advance doctrines without examining principles. Why do I gaze on the Cupid of Praxiteles? because it is beautiful; because it gives me pleasurable sensations. If it gave me no pleasurable sensations, should I find it beautiful? should I gaze upon it? or would you call me wise if then I gave a drachma for its possession? What other means have we of judging of things than by the effect they produce upon our senses? Our senses then being the judges of all things, the aim of all men is to gratify their senses; in other words, their aim is pleasure or happiness: and if virtue were not found to conduce to this, men would do well to shun her, as they now do well to shun vice."

"You own then no pleasure but virtue, and no misery but vice?"

"Not at all: I think virtue only the highest pleasure, and vice, or ungoverned passions and appetites, the worst misery. Other pleasures are requisite to form a state of perfect ease, which is happiness; and other miseries are capable of troubling, perhaps destroying, the peace of the most virtuous and the wisest man."

"I begin to see more reason in your doctrine," said the youth, looking up with a timid blush in the face of the philosopher.

"And less monstrous depravity," replied the Gargettian, laughing, "My young friend," he continued, more seriously, "learn henceforth to form your judgments upon knowledge, not report. Credulity is always a ridiculous, often a dangerous failing: it has made of many a clever man, a fool; and of many a good man, a knave. But have you nothing to urge against me? You say you see more reason in my doctrine, which implies, that you think me less wrong, but not right."

"I am a young disputant," answered Theon, "and very unfit to engage with such a master."

"That does not follow; a bad logician may have a good understanding; and a young mind may be an acute one. If my argument have truth in it, less than a philosopher will see it; and if it have not, less than a logician may refute it."

"I think I could urge some objections," replied Theon; "but they are so confused and indistinct, I almost fear to bring them forth."

"I dare say I could forestall the most of them," said the master. "But I had rather leave your mind to its own exercise. Think over the matter at leisure, and you shall start your questions some evening or morning among my scholars. Knowledge is better imparted in a dialogue than a lecture; and a dialogue is not the worse for having more than two interlocutors. So! our walk has well ended with our subject. Let us see what friends are here. There are surely voices."

Their route had been circular, and had brought them again in front of the temple. "This is a favorite lodgment of mine," said the sage, ascending the noble flight of steps and entering the open door. The apartment, spacious, vaulted, and circular, occupied the whole of the building. The walls were adorned with fine copies of the best pieces of Zeuxis and Parrhasius, and some beautiful originals of Apelles. A statue, the only one in the apartment, was raised on a pedestal in the centre. It was a Venus Urania, by the hand of Lysippus, well chosen as the presiding deity in the gardens of virtuous pleasure. The ceiling, rising into a noble dome, represented the heavens — a ground of deep blue; the stars, sun, and planets, in raised gold. But two living figures soon fixed the attention of Theon. In one he recognized Metrodorus, though he had not the evening before much observed his countenance. He stood at a painter's easel. His figure was more graceful than dignified, his face more expressive than handsome. The eyes, dark, piercing, and brilliant, were bent in a painter's earnest gaze on his living study. The forehead was short, raised much at the temples, and singularly over the brows. The hair of a dark glossy brown, short and curled. The cheeks at the moment deeply flushed with the eagerness, and, perhaps, the impatience of an artist. The mouth curled voluptuously, yet not without a mixture of satire; the chin curved upwards, slightly Grecian, assisted this expression. His study was Leontium. She stood, rather than leaned, against a pilaster of the wall; one arm supported on a slab of marble, an unrolled book half lying on the same, and half in her opened hand. The other arm, partly hid in the drapery, dropped loosely by her side. Her fine face turned a little over the left shoulder, to meet the eye of the painter. Not a muscle played; the lips seemed not to breathe: so calm, so pale, so motionless — she looked a statue; so noble, so severely beautiful — she looked the Minerva of Phidias.

"I cannot do it!" cried Metrodorus, flinging down his pencil. "I had need be Apelles, to take that face." He pushed back his easel in disgust.

"What!" said Leontium, her fine features relaxing into a heavenly smile, "and is all my patience to go for nothing?"

"I am a blundering, blind Boeotian! a savage Spartan!" continued the disappointed artist. "There!" and seizing a brush, was about to demolish his work.

"For your life!" cried Leontium; and starting forward, pulled aside his hand. "Oh, the mad ill-temper of a genius! Why, friend, if my face were half so fine as that, Juno would be jealous of it."

"And who knows that she is not? A daub! a vile daub!" still muttered the impatient scholar, yet his face gradually relaxing its anger, as in spite of itself, till it turned to meet Leontium's with a smile.

"And there stand the master and the young Corinthian laughing at you," said Leontium.

They approached. "Are you a judge?" asked Metrodorus of Theon.

"I am afraid not, though the confession will mar my compliments."

"But I am," said the Gargettian, humorously: "and though I have all the inclination in the world, yet I cannot quarrel with the performance. Well outlined and finely coloured. The attitude and air hit exactly. The features too. Perhaps — the only possible perhaps my ill-nature can stumble on —– perhaps the expression is too blooming, and less mental than that of the original."

"Why there — there it is!" cried the scholar, his face resuming all its vexation. "The look of an idiot instead of a genius."

"Not quite that either: only of a Hebe instead of a Juno. More like our Hedeia."

"Like a monster!" muttered the angry artist.

"Oh Hercules, oh Hercules!" cried the sage. "What it is to rub a sore place! Better break a man's leg than blow a feather on his razed shin. Had I (turning to Theon) told him he had drawn a hump-backed Thersites he would have blessed me, rather than for this pretty compliment of a blooming-faced Hebe."

"I might as well have done one as the other; they were equally like the original."

"I must bow to that compliment," said Leontium, laying her hand on her breast, and inclining with affected gravity to the painter.

He tried in vain to resist the laugh: then looking to the master — "What would you have me turn it to?"

"As you object to a Hebe, to a philosopher by all means. Silver the head a little, it may be an admirable Epicurus."

"Nay! don't make the madman furious," said Leontium, placing her hand on Metrodorus's shoulder; then addressing Theon, "Pray, young man, if you want to be a philosopher, never find an eye for painting, a finger for music, or a brain for poetry. Any one of these will keep a man from wisdom."

"But not a woman, I suppose," retorted Metrodorus, "as you have all three."

"Ready at compliments this morning: but if you wanted a bow for this, you should have given it with a more gracious face. But come, my poor friend; we will try and put you in good humor — nothing like a little flattery for this. Here, my young Corinthian! (walking to the other side of the room to a newly finished picture that stood against the wall, and beckoning Theon towards her,) you may without skill perceive the beauty of this work, and the excellence of the likeness."

It was indeed striking. "Admirable!" cried Theon, after a long gaze of admiration, and then turning to compare it with the original.

"A little flattered, and more than a little, I fear," said Epicurus with a smile, as he moved towards them.

"Flattered!" exclaimed Metrodorus; a Parrhasius could not flatter such an original."

"You see how my scholars spoil me," said the Gargettian to Theon.

"But you think," continued Metrodorus, " that I have done it common justice."

"Much more than common: — It is your
Master's self. The dignity of his figure, the
grace of his attitude, the nobility of his
features, the divine benignity of his
expression. Had we not the original to
worship, we might worship your copy."

They were interrupted by the entrance of a
crowd of disciples, in the midst of whose
salutations young Sofron rushed in, breathless
with running and convulsed with laughter.

CHAPTER IV.

"Prepare yourselves! prepare yourselves!" cried the panting scholar. "Oh, Pollux, such a couple! The contrast might convulse a Scythian."

"What is it? What is the matter? cried a dozen voices. "I'll explain directly — give me breath — and yet I must be quick, for they are close on my heels. Gryphus, the cynic – some of you must have seen him. Well he's coming side by side with young Lycaon."

"Coming here," said the master, smiling. "What can have procured me the honor of such a visit?"

"O, your fame of course."

"I suspect you are making a fool of the old Cynic," said Epicurus.

"Nay, if he be a fool, he is one without my assistance: Lycaon and I were standing on the steps of the Prytaneum, disputing about something, I forget what, when by came Gryphus, and stopping short at bottom of the steps, 'Are you disciples of Epicurus, of Gargettium? 'We are,' answered I, for Lycaon only stood staring in amazement. 'You may show me the way to him then.' ' With all my heart,' I again replying, Lycaon not yet finding his tongue. 'We are at present for the gardens, and shall hold it an honor to be conductors to so extraordinary a personage.' I wanted to put him between us, but Lycaon seemed unambitious of his share in this distinction, for, stepping back, he slipped round to my other side. Oh, Jupiter! I shall never forget the contrast between my two companions. The pale, dirty, hairy cynic on my right hand, and the fine, smooth, delicate, pretty Aristippian on my left. We brought the whole street at our heels. Lycaon would have slunk away, but I held him tight by the sleeve. When we were fairly in the gardens, I gave them the slip at a cross-path, and run on before to give timely notice, as you see. But lo! Behold!"

The two figures now appeared at the door. The contrast was not much less singular than the scholar had represented; and there was a sort of a faint prelude to a universal laugh, which, however, a timely look from the master instantly quelled. Lycaon, from the lightness of his figure, and delicacy of his features and complexion, might have been mistaken for a female; his skin had the whiteness of the lily, and the blushing red of the rose ; his lips the vermil of coral: his hair soft and flowing; in texture, silk; in color, gold: his dress was chosen with studied nicety, and disposed with studied elegance: the tunic of the whitest and finest linen, fastened at the shoulder with a beautiful onyx: the sash of exquisite embroidery, and the robe of the richest Tyrian, falling in luxuriant folds from the shoulders, and over the right arm which gracefully sustained its length, for the greater convenience in walking: the sandals purple, with buttons of gold. Gryphus, short, square, and muscular; his tunic of the coarsest and not the cleanest woollen, in some places worn threadbare, and with one open rent of considerable magnitude, that proved the skin to be as well engrained as its covering : his girdle, a rope: his cloak, or rather rag, had the appearance of a sail taken from the wreck of an old trader: his feet bare, and thickly powdered with dust: of his face, little more might be distinguished than the nose; the lower part being obscured by a bushy and wide-spreading beard, and the upper, by a profusion of long, tangled, and grisly hair. The wondering disciples opened a passage for this singular intruder, who, without looking to the right or the left, walked on, and stopped before Epicurus.

"I suppose you are the master, by the needless trouble I see you take, in coming to meet me."

"When Gryphus has possibly walked a mile to meet Epicurus, Epicurus may without much trouble walk a step to meet Gryphus."

"In my walk of a mile," returned the cynic, " there was no trouble: I took it for my own pleasure."

"And my walk of a step I also took for mine."

"Aye, the pleasure of ceremony!"

"I may hope then this your visit is from something more than ceremony — perhaps a feeling of real friendship, or as a mark of your good opinion."

"I hate useless words," returned the cynic, "and am not come here either to make any, or hearken to any. I have heard you much talked of lately. Our streets and our porticos buzz eternally with your name, till now all wise men are weary of it. I come to tell you this, and to advise you to shut the gates of your gardens forthwith, and to cease the harangues of a master, since you only pass for a philosopher among fools, and for a fool among philosophers."

"I thank you for your honest advice and information, friend; but as the object of a master is not to teach the wise, but only the unwise, do you not think I may still harangue among fools to some little purpose, though Gryphus, and all sages, will of course justly hold me in contempt?"

"And so that fools may be made wise, the wise are to be plagued with folly?"

"Nay, you would surely cease to think that folly which could make a fool wise."

"A fool wise! And who but a fool would think that possible?"

"I grant it were difficult; but may it not also

sometimes be difficult to discover who is a fool, and who not? Among my scholars there, some doubtless may be fools, and some possibly may not be fools."

"No, interrupted the cynic, "or they would not be your scholars."

"Ah! I being a fool myself. Well reminded! I had forgot that was one of our premises. But then, I being a fool, and all my scholars being fools, I do not see how much harm can be done, either by my talking folly or their hearkening to it."

"No, if wise men were not forced to hearken also. I tell you, that our streets and our porticos buzz with your name and your nonsense. Keep all the fools of Athens in your gardens, and lock the gates, and you may preach folly as long and as loud as you please."

"I have but one objection to this, namely, that my gardens would not hold all the fools of Athens. Suppose, therefore, the wise men, being a smaller body, were shut into a garden, and the city and the rest of Attica left for the fools."

"I told you," cried the cynic, in a voice of anger, "that I hated useless words."

"Nay, friend, why then walk a mile to speak advice to me? No words so useless as those thrown at a fool."

"Very true, very true;" and so saying, the stranger turned his back and quitted the temple.

"There," said the son of Neocles to his smiling disciples, "is a good warning to any, or all of us, who would be philosophers."

"Nay, master," cried Sofron, "do you think us in danger of following the pleasant example of this savage? Do you, indeed, expect to see Lycaon there, with beard, head, and clothing, after the fashion of Gryphus?"

"Not beard, head, and clothing, perhaps," answered the Gargettian, "pride, vanity, and ambition, may take less fearful coverings than these."

"Pride, vanity, and ambition? I should rather suspect Gryphus of the want of all three."

"Nay, my son, believe me, all those three qualities were concerned in the carving of those three frightful appendages of our cynic's person. Pride need not always lead a man to cut mount Athos in two, like Xerxes; nor ambition, to conquer a world, and weep that there is yet not another to conquer, like Alexander; nor vanity, to look in a stream at his own face till he fall in love with it, like Narcissus. When we cannot cut an Athos, we may leave uncut our beard; when we cannot mount a throne, we may crawl into a tub; and when we have no beauty, we may increase our ugliness. If a man of small, or even of moderate talents, be smitten with a great desire of distinction, there is nothing too absurd, perhaps nothing too mischievous, for him too commit. Our friend, the cynic, happily for himself and his neighbors, seems disposed to rest with the absurd. Erostratus took to the mischievous — to eternize his name destroying that temple, by the building of which Etesiphon immortalized his. Be it our care to keep equally clear of the one as the other."

"Do you then," asked Theon, "think a desire of distinction a vicious desire?"

"I think it is often a dangerous desire, and very often an unhappy one."

"But surely very often a fortunate one," said Leontium. "Without it, would there ever have been a hero?"

"And perhaps," returned the sage, with a smile, "the world might have been as happy if there had not."

"Well, without arguing for an Achilles, would there have been a Homer?"

"I agree with you," replied the master, more seriously. "The desire of distinction, though often a dangerous, and often an unhappy desire, is likewise often, though I believe here *sometimes* were a better word, a fortunate one. It is dangerous in the head of a fool; unhappy, in that of a man of moderate abilities, or unfavorable situation, who can conceive a noble aim, but lacks the talent or the means necessary for its attainment. It is fortunate only in the head of a genius, the heart of a sage, and in a situation convenient for its development and gratification. These three things you will allow do not often meet in one person."

"Yet," said Theon, "how many great men has Athens produced."

"But it is not a consequent that they were happy."

"Happy or not happy, who would refuse their fate?"

"I like that feeling," replied the Gargettian; "nor do I dissent from it. The fate of greatness will always be enviable, even when the darkest storms trouble its course. Well-merited fame has in itself a pleasure so much above all pleasures, that it may weigh in the balance against all the accumulated evils of mortality. Grant, then, our great men to have been fortunate; are they, as you say, so many? Alas! my son, we may count them on our fingers. A generation, the most brilliant in genius, leaves out of its thousands and millions but three or four, or a dozen, to the worship, even to the knowledge of futurity."

"And these, only these three, four, or a dozen, have a right to the desire of distinction?"

"As to the right," replied the sage playfully, "I mean not to dispute that. The right lies with all men in our democracy to sit in a tub, or to walk in a dirty tunic."
"But you will allow of no end in ambition but an absurd one."

"I have not expressed myself well, or you have not understood me well, if you draw that conclusion. I surely have granted our great men to have had great ends of ambition."

"But is it only great men, or men destined to be great, that may have such ends?"

"I allowed that others might; I only said that they would be unhappy in consequence. The perfection of wisdom, and the end of true philosophy, is to proportion our wants to our possessions, our ambitions to our capacities."

"Then," cried Metrodorus, "I have substantially proved myself this morning to be no philosopher, when I chose a study beyond the reach of my pencil."

"No," said Leontium, playfully tapping his shoulder, "the master will make a distinction between what is beyond the reach of our capacity, and what beyond the reach of our practice. Erostratus might *never* have planned the edifice he destroyed; Ctesiphon could not *always* have planned it." The smile that accompanied these words, lighted one yet more brilliant in the face of Metrodorus. Theon guessed that he felt more than admiration and more than friendship, for this female disciple.

"Your remark was well timed and well pointed," said the master, " and has saved me some talking."

"I am not sure of that," cried Sofron, stepping forwards; "for though Leontium has so nicely worded the distinction between want of capacity and want of practice in the general, I should like to be told, how a man is to make this distinction between his own in particular? For instance, I have a fancy to turn philosopher, and supersede my master; how am I to tell, at my first non-plus in logic or invention, whether the defect be in my capacity or my practice."

"If it be only in the last, I apprehend you will easily perceive it; if in the first, not so readily. A man, if he set about the search, will quickly discover his talents; he may continue it to his death without discovering his deficiencies. The reason is plain: the one hurts our self-love, the other flatters it."

"And yet," interrupted Theon, "I think, in my first interview with the philosopher of Gargettium, he remarked, that thousands had the seeds of excellence in them, who never found them out."

"I see you have a good memory," returned the master. "I did say so, and I think it still. Many might have been heroes, and many philosophers, had they had a desire to be either; had accident or ambition made them look into themselves, and inquire into their powers; but though jewels be hid in a sack of oats, they will never be found, unless the oats be shaken. Remember, however, we are now speaking of one class of men only — the ambitious; and the ambitious will never have any seeds in them, bad or good, that will not generate and produce their proper fruit. Ambition is the spur, and the necessary spur of a great mind to great action; when acting upon a weak mind it impels it to absurdity, or sours it with discontent."

"Nay, then," said Sofron, " 'tis but a dangerous inmate, as minds go; and I, for one, had better have none of it, for I doubt I am not born to be an Epicurus, and I am certain I have no inclination to be a Gryphus."

"Well," said the master, "we have at least to thank Gryphus for our morning's dialogue. If any of us wish to prosecute it farther, we may do it over our repast — the sun has reached his noon, so let us to the bath."

They left the temple, and crossing the gardens in an opposite direction from that by which Theon had entered, soon reached a gate, which, to his surprise, opened on a court at the back of the Gargettian's house, the same in which he had supped the preceding evening.

CHAPTER V.

The fervors of the day had declined, when Theon issued to the street from the house of Epicurus: at that instant he met in the face his friend Cleanthes: he ran to his embrace; but the young stoic, receding with mingled astonishment and horror — "Ye gods! from the house of Epicurus?"

"I do not marvel at your surprise," returned Theon, "nor, if I recall my own feelings of yesterday, at your indignation."

"Answer me quickly," interrupted Cleanthes; "is Theon yet my friend?"

"And does Cleanthes doubt it?"

"What may I not doubt, when I see you come from such a mansion?"

"Nay, my brother," said Theon, kindly throwing his arm round the neck of his friend, and drawing him onwards, "I have been in no mansion of vice, or of folly."
"I do not understand you," returned the stoic, but half yielding to his kindness: "I do not

know what to think or what to fear."

"Fear nothing, and think only good," said the Corinthian. "True, I come from the gardens of pleasure, where I have heard very little of pleasure, and a very great deal of virtue."

"I see how it is," returned the other, "you have lost your principles, and I, my friend."

"I do not think I have lost the first, and I am very sure you have not lost the last."

"No!" exclaimed Cleanthes; "but I tell you, yes;" and his cheeks flushed, and his eyes flashed with indignation: "I *have* lost my friend, and you have lost yours. Go!" he continued, and drew himself from the arm of Theon. "Go! Cleanthes has no fellowship with an apostate and libertine."

"You wrong me, and you wrong Epicurus," said his friend, in a tone of more reproach than anger. "But I cannot blame you; yesterday I had myself been equally unjust. You must see him, you must hear him, Cleanthes. This alone can undeceive you — can convince you; convince you of my innocence and Epicurus' virtue."

"Epicurus' virtue? your innocence? "What is Epicurus to me? What is he, or should he be to you? Your innocence? And is this fastened to the mantle of Epicurus? See him to be convinced of your innocence?"

"Yes, and of your own injustice. Oh, Cleanthes, what a fool do I now know myself to have been! To have listened to the lies of Timocrates! To have believed all his absurdities! Come, my friend! come with me, and behold the face of the master he blasphemes!"

"Theon, one master, and but one master, is mine. To me, whether Timocrates exaggerate or even lie, it matters nothing."

"It does, or it should," said the Corinthian. "Will a disciple of Zeno not open his eyes to truth? Not see an error, and atone for it, by acknowledging it? I do not ask you to be the disciple of Epicurus — I only ask you to be just to him, and that for your own sake, more than mine, or even his."

"I see you are seduced — I see you are lost,"
cried the stoic, fixing on him a look, in which
sorrow struggled with indignation. "I thought
myself a stoic, but I feel the weakness of a
woman in my eyes. Thou wert as my brother,
Theon; and thou — thou also art beguiled by
the Syren — left virtue for pleasure, Zeno for
Epicurus."

"I have not left Zeno."

"You cannot follow both — you cannot be in
the day and under the night at one and the
same time."

"I tell you, there is no night in the gardens of
Epicurus."

"Is there no pleasure there," cried the stoic, his
mouth and brows curling with irony.

"Yes, there is pleasure there: the pleasure of
wisdom and virtue."

"Ah! have you learnt the Gargettian subtleties
so soon? You have doubtless already
worshiped virtue under the form of the
courtezan Leontium; and wisdom under that

of her master and paramour, the son of Neocles."

"How little you know of either," returned Theon! " But I knew as little yesterday."

Cleanthes stopped. They were before the stoic portico." Farewell! Return to your gardens! Farewell!"

"We do not yet part," said Theon: Zeno is still my master." He followed his friend up the steps. A crowd of disciples were assembled, waiting the arrival of their master. Some, crowded into groups, listened to the harangues of an elder or more able scholar: others walking in parties of six or a dozen, reasoning, debating, and disputing: while innumerable single figures, undisturbed by the buzz around them, leaned against the pillars, studying each from a manuscript, or stood upon the steps with arms folded, and heads dropped on their bosoms, wrapped in silent meditations. At the entrance of Cleanthes, the favored pupil of their master, the scholars made way, and the loud hum slowly hushed into silence. He advanced to the centre, and the floating crowd gathered and compressed into a wide and deep circle. All eyes bent on the youth in expectant curiosity, for his countenance was disturbed, and his manner abrupt.

Cleanthes was of the middle size: so slender, that you wondered at the erectness of his gait and activity of his motion. His neck was small; his shoulders falling; his head elegantly-formed; the hair smooth and close cut; the forehead narrow, and somewhat deeply lined for one so young: the eye-brows marked and even, save a slight bend upwards as by a frown, above the nose. The eyes blue: but their gaze was too earnest, and their spirit too clear, to leave any of the melting softness so usual with that color: — and yet there were moments when this would appear in them; and when it did, it went to the soul of him who observed it; but such moments were short and rare. The nose was finely and perhaps too delicately turned: the mouth, mild and always in repose. The cheeks were thin, and though slightly flushed, the face had a look of paleness till enthusiasm awoke, and deepened all its dyes. The whole expression had more spirituality and variety, and the manner more agitation, than you would have

looked for in the first and favorite pupil of
Zeno. The youth turned a rapid glance round
the circle: he threw out his right arm; the
mantle dropped from his shoulder, and in a
varied, piercing, and yet melodious voice, he
began —

"My friends! my brothers! disciples of Zeno
and of virtue! Give me your ears, and awake
your faculties! How shall I tell the dangers
that surround you? How shall I paint the
demon that would ensnare you? Timocrates
hath escaped from his enchantments, and told
us that riot and reveling were in his halls, that
impiety was in his mouth; vice in his practice;
deformity in his aspect: and we thought that
none but souls born for error, already steeped
in infamy, or sunk in effeminacy, could be
taken in his toils and seduced by his example.
But behold! he hath changed his countenance
— he hath changed his tongue: amid his
revels he hath put on the garb of decency: in
his riot he talks of innocence; in his
licentiousness of virtue! Behold the youth!
they run to him with greedy ears — they
throng his gardens and his porticoes. Athens,
Attica, Greece, all are the Gargettian's. Asia,
Italy, the burning Afric and the frozen Scythia

— all, all send ready pupils to his feet. Oh! what shall we say? Oh! how shall we stem the torrent! Oh! how shall we fence our hearts — how our ears from the song of the Syren. To what mast shall we bind ourselves, to what pilot shall we trust, that we may pass the shores in safety without dashing on the rocks? But why do I speak? Why do I inquire? Why do I exhort: Is not the contagion already among us? In the school of Zeno — in this portico — in this circle are there not waverers? Yea, are there not apostates?" Emotion choked his utterance: he paused, and glanced his kindled eyes round upon the audience. Every breath was held in expectation; each looked on the other in doubt, dismay, and inquiry. Theon's heart beat quick and high: he advanced one step, and raised his arm to speak: but Cleanthes, gathering his breath, again in a rapid voice continued.

Does this silence speak conscious guilt, or startled innocence? The last: I will believe the last. Praise be to the gods! praise to our guardian, Minerva! praise to our great, our glorious master, there are yet some sons left to Athens and to Greece, who shall respect, follow, and attain to virtue! Some choice and disciplined souls, who shall stand forth the light and ornament of their age, and whose names shall be in honor with those yet unborn. Rouse, rouse up your energies! Oh, be firm, to Zeno, and to virtue! I tell you not — Zeno tells you not, that virtue is founded in pleasure and repose. Resistance, energy, watchfulness, patience, and endurance — these, these must be your practice, must be your habit, ere you can reach the perfection of your nature. The ascent is steep, is long, is arduous. To-day you must ascend a step, and to-morrow a step, and to-morrow, and to-morrow — and yet shall you be far from the summit, from rest, and from security. Does this appall you? Does this disgust you? Go then to the gardens. Go to the man of Gargettium — he who calls himself philosopher, and who loves and teaches folly! Go, go to him, and he shall encourage and soothe you. He shall end your pursuit, and give you your ambition! lie shall show you virtue robed in pleasures, and lolling in ease! lie shall teach you wisdom in a song, and happiness in impiety! But I am told, that Timocrates has lied; that Epicurus is not a libertine; nor Leontium a prostitute; nor the youth of the garden the ministers to their lusts. Be it so. Timocrates must answer to himself, whether his tale be the outpourings of indignant truth, or the subtle inventions of malevolence: with his own conscience be the secret: to us it matters nothing. We, who have nought to do with the doctrines of Epicurus, have nought to do with his practice. Let him who would vindicate the one, vindicate the other: let him come forth and say, that the master in the gardens is not only pure in action, but perfect in theory. Let him say, that he worships virtue as virtue, and shuns vice as vice. Let him say, that he arms the soul with fortitude, ennobles it with magnanimity, chastens it with temperance, enlarges it with beneficence, perfects it with justice: — and let him moreover say, that he does this, not that the soul so schooled and invigorated may lie in the repose of virtue, but that it may exult in its honor, and be fitted for its activity. Fie on that virtue which prudence alone directs! Which teaches to be just that the laws may not punish, or our neighbors revenge: to be enduring — because complainings were useless, and weakness would bring on us insult and contempt: — to be temperate — that our body may keep its vigor, our appetites retain their acuteness, and our gratifications and sensualities their zest: — to serve our friends — that they may serve us; — our country — because its defense and well-being comprehends our own. Why, all this is well — but is there nothing more? Is it our ease alone we shall study, and not our dignity? Though all my fellow-men were swept away, and not a mortal nor immortal eye were left to approve or condemn — should I not here — within this breast, have a judge to dread, and a friend to conciliate? Prudence and pleasure! Was it from such principles as these, that the virtue of Solon, of Miltiades, of Aristides, of Socrates, of Plato, of Xenophon, of all our heroes and all our sages, had its spring and its nourishment? Was it such virtue as this that in Lycurgus put by the offered crown? that in Leonidas stood at Thermopylae? that in the dying Pericles gloried that he had never caused a citizen to mourn? Was it such virtue as this, that spoke in Socrates before his judges? that sustained him in his prison, and when the door was open, and the sails of the ready ship unfurled, made him prefer death to flight; his dignity to his existence?"

Again the young orator paused, but his indignant soul seemed still to speak from his flashing eyes. His cheeks glowed as fire, and the big drops rolled from his forehead. At this moment the circle behind him gave way, and Zeno advanced into the midst: he stood by the head and shoulders above the crowd: his breast, broad and manly; his limbs, cast in strength and symmetry: his gait, erect, calm, and dignified: his features, large, grand, and regular, seemed sculptured by the chisel for a colossal divinity: the forehead, broad and serene, was marked with the even lines of wisdom and age; but no harsh wrinkles nor playing muscles disturbed the repose of his cheeks, nor had sixty years touched with one thread of silver his close black hair: the eyes, dark, and full, fringed with long strait lashes, looked in severe and steady wisdom from under their correct and finely arched brows : the nose came from the forehead, strait and even: the mouth and chin were firm and silent. Wisdom undisturbable, fortitude unshakeable, self-respect, self-possession, and self-knowledge perfected, were in his face, his carriage, and his tread.

He stopped before the youth, who had turned

at his approach. "My son," fixing his calm gaze on the working countenance of his pupil, "what hath disturbed thy soul?"' Cleanthes laid a hand on his laboring breast: he made one violent effort for composure and speech: it failed. The hot blood forsook his cheeks: it rushed again: again it fled: he gasped, and dropped fainting at the feet of his master.

CHAPTER VI.

Theon rushed forward: he knelt; he raised the
head of his friend: breathless, agitated,
terrified, he called his name with the piercing
cry of agony and despair. All was commotion
and confusion. The scholar's pressed forward
tumultuously; but Zeno, raising his arm, and
looking steadily round, cried "Silence!" The
crowd fell back, and the stillness of night
succeeded. Then motioning the circle towards
the street, to give way and admit the air, he
stooped and assisted Theon to support his
reviving pupil. Cleanthes raised his head,
turned his eyes wildly around, and then fixed
them on his master.

"Gently," said Zeno, as the youth struggled in
their arms for recollection, "gently, my son."
But he made the effort: he gained his feet, and
throwing out his arm to a pillar neat him,
turned his head aside, and for some moments
combated with his weakness in silence. His
limbs still trembled, and his face had yet the
hues of death, when, pressing his hand with
convulsive strength against the pillar, he
proudly drew up his form, turned his eyes
again upon his master, and mustering his

broken respiration—"Blame me, but do not despise me."

"I shall do neither, my son: the weakness was in the body, not the mind."

"There has been want of command in both. I ask not to be excused." Then turning round to his companions, "I may be a warning, if not an example. The Spartans expose the drunkenness of their Helots to confirm their youth in sobriety: let the weakness of Cleanthes teach the sons of Zeno equanimity; and let them say, — if in the portico weakness be found, what shall it be in the gardens? But," he continued, addressing his master, "will Zeno pardon the scholar, who, while enforcing his nervous doctrines on others, has swerved from them himself?"

"Thou judgest thy fault as thou shouldst judge it," returned Zeno; "but comfort, my son! He who knows, and knowing can acknowledge his deficiency, though his foot be not on the summit, yet hath he his eye there. But say the cause, and surely it must be a great one, that could disturb the self-possession of my disciple."

"The cause was indeed a great one; no less than the apostacy of a scholar from Zeno to Epicurus."

Zeno turned his eyes round the circle: there was no additional severity in them, and no change in his manner, or in his deep sonorous voice, when, addressing them, he said, "If one, or more, or all of my disciples, be wearied of virtue, let them depart. Let them not fear upbraidings or exhortations; the one were useless to you, the other unworthy of me. He who sighs for pleasure, the voice of wisdom can never reach, nor the power of virtue touch. In this portico truth will never be softened to win a sickly ear; nor the severity of virtue, will it ever be veiled to win a feeble heart. He who obeys in act and not in thought; he who disciplines his body and not his mind; he who hath his foot in the portico, and his heart in the gardens; he hath no more to do with Zeno, than a wretch sunk in all the effeminacy of a Median, or the gross debauchery of a Scythian. There is no mid-way in virtue; no halting place for the soul but perfection. You must be all, or you may be nothing. You must determine to proceed to the utmost, or I encourage ye not to begin. I say to ye, one and all, give me your ears, your understandings, your souls, and your energies, or *depart*!" Again he looked round upon his scholars. A long and deep silence succeeded: when young Theon, breaking through his awe and his timidity, advanced into the centre, and craving sufferance with his hand, addressed the assembly.

"Though I should forfeit the esteem of Zeno and the love of his disciples, I have no choice but to speak. Honor and justice demand this of me: first to remove suspicion from this assembly; next, to vindicate the character of a sage, whom the tongue of a liar hath traduced; and, lastly, to conciliate my own esteem, which I value beyond even the esteem of the venerated Zeno, and of my beloved Cleanthes." He paused, and turning to Zeno —"With permission of the master, I would speak."

"Speak, my son: we attend." Zeno retreated among his disciples; and Cleanthes, anxious and agitated for his friend, placed himself behind the screen of a pillar. With a varying cheek and tremulous voice, the youth began:

"In addressing an assembly accustomed to the manly elocution of a Zeno, and the glowing eloquence of a Cleanthes, I know I shall be forgiven by my companions, and I hope even by my severe master, the blushes and hesitations of timidity and inexperience. I open my mouth for the first time in public; and in what a public is it? Let not, therefore, my confusion be thought the confusion of guilt; but, as it truly is, of bashful inexperience. First, to remove suspicion from this assembly: — let not the scholars look with doubt on each other; let not the master look with doubt on his scholars. I am he who have communed with the son of Neocles; I am he who have entered the gardens of pleasure; I am he whom Cleanthes hath pointed at as the apostate from Zeno to Epicurus." A tumult arose among the scholars. Surprise, indignation, and scorn, variously looked from their faces, and murmured from their tongues.

"Silence!" cried Zeno, casting his severe glance round the circle. "Young man, proceed."

This burst of his audience rather invigorated than dashed the youth. He freely threw forth his arm; his eyes lighted with fire, and the ready words flowed from his lips. "I merit not the hiss of scorn, nor the burst of indignation. Desist, my brothers, till my artless tale be told; till you have heard, not my apology, but my justification. Yesterday, at this hour, I left the portico, heated to fury by the philippic of Timocrates against Epicurus and his disciples; indignant at the city that did not drive such a teacher from its walls; against the gods, who did not strike him with their thunders. Thus venting my feelings in soliloquy, after a long ramble I seated myself on the banks of Cephisus, and was awakened from a reverie by the approach of a stranger: his aspect had the wisdom of a sage, and the benignity of a divinity. I yielded him the homage of youthful respect and admiration: he condescended to address me. He gave me the precepts of virtue with the gentle and honied tongue of kindness and persuasion. I listened, I admired, and I loved. We did not conclude our walk until sunset: he bade me to his supper. I entered his house, and he told me I beheld Epicurus. Could I have drawn back? Should I have drawn back? No: my heart answers, no. Your sufferance my friends! Do not interrupt me! Do not call me an apostate! In the presence of the gods; in the presence of my master, whom I fear as them; in the presence of my own conscience, which I fear more than both, I swear that I am not so! I mean not to explain or to justify the philosophy of Epicurus: I know but little of it. I only know — I only affirm, that his tongue has given new warmth to my love of virtue, and new vigor to my pursuit of it. I only affirm, that persuasion, simple, ungarnished persuasion, is on his lips; benevolence in his aspect; urbanity in his manners; generosity, truth, and candor, in his sentiments; I only affirm, that order, innocence, and content, are in his halls and his gardens; peace and brotherly love with his disciples; and that, in the midst of these, he is himself the philosopher, the parent, and the friend. I see the sneer of contempt upon your lips, my brothers; alas! even on the unperturbed countenance of my master I read displeasure."

"No, my son," said Zeno, "thou dost not. Continue thy artless tale. If there be error, it lies with the deceiver, not the deceived. And you, my sons and disciples, banish from your faces and your breasts every expression and every thought unworthy of your honest companion, and your upright sect. For remember, if to abhor falsehood and vice be noble, to distrust truth and innocence is mean. My son, proceed."

"Thanks for your noble confidence, my master: it makes me proud, for I deserve it. Yes! even should I, as I perceive you apprehend, be deceived, I feel that this open confession of my present perfect conviction is honorable both to myself and to Zeno. It proves that in his school I have learnt candor, though I have yet to learn discernment. And yet, methinks, however imperfect my youthful discernment, it is not now in error. If ever I saw simple, unadorned goodness; if ever I heard simple, unadorned truth, it is in, it is from Epicurus. Again your sufferance, my friends! Again your sufferance, my master! I am not — I wish not to be, a disciple of the gardens: virtue may be in them — excuse me, virtue *is* in them; but there is a virtue in the portico which I shall worship to my latest hour. Here, here I first learned — here I first saw to what a glorious height of greatness a mortal might ascend — how independent he might be of fortune; how triumphant over fate! Young, innocent, and inexperienced, I came to Athens in search of wisdom and virtue. 'Attend all the schools, and fix with that which shall give you the noblest aims,' said my father, when he gave me his parting blessing. He being an academician, I had, of course, somewhat imbibed the principles of Plato, and conceived a love for his school. On first hearing Crates, therefore, I thought myself satisfied. Accident made me acquainted with a young Pythagorean: I listened to his simple precepts; I loved his virtues, and almost fell into his superstitions. From these Theophrastes awakened me; and I was nearly fixed as a Peripatetic, when I met the eloquent, enthusiastic Cleanthes. He brought me to the portico, where I found all the virtues of all the schools united, and crowned with perfection. But when I preferred Zeno, I did not despise my former masters. I still sometimes visit the lyceum and the academy, and still the young Pythagoraen is my friend. A pure mind should, I think, respect virtue wherever it be found: and if then in the lyceum and the academy, why not in the gardens? Zeno, in teaching austerity, does not teach intolerance; much less, I am sure, does he teach ingratitude: and if I did not feel for the sage of Gargettium both respect and love, I were the most ungrateful soul in Athens; and if, feeling both, I feared to acknowledge both, I were the meanest. And now, my brothers, ask yourselves what would be your indignation at the youth, who for his vices being driven from this portico, should run to the lyceum, and accuse, to the sons of Aristotle, our great Zeno of that sensuality and wickedness which had here wrought his own disgrace, and his own banishment? Would ye not hate such a wretch? Would ye not loathe him? Would ye not curse him? My brothers! this day have I learned such a wretch to be Timocrates. Is he here? I hope he is. I hope he hears me denounce him for a defamer and an ingrate."

"'Tis false!" cried Timocrates, bursting in fury from the crowd. "'Tis false! I swear" —

"Beware of perjury!" said a clear, silver voice, from without the circle." Give way, Athenians! 'Tis for me to take up this quarrel."

The crowd divided. Every eye turned towards the opening. Theon shouted with triumph; Timocrates stood blank with dismay — for they recognized the voice and the form of the son of Neocles.

CHAPTER VII.

The sage advanced towards Theon: he laid a hand on either of his shoulders, and kissed his glowing forehead. "Thanks to my generous defender. Your artless tale, my son, if it have not gained the ear of Zeno, hath fixed the heart of Epicurus. Oh, ever keep this candor and this innocence!" He turned his benign face round the circle: "Athenians! I am Epicurus."

This name, so despised and execrated, did it not raise a tumult in the assembly? No; every tongue was chained, every breath suspended, every eye rivetted with wonder and admiration. Theon had said the truth: it was the aspect of a sage and a divinity. The face was a serene mirror of a serene mind: its expression spoke like music to the soul, Zeno's was not more calm and unruffled; but here was no severity, no authority, no reserve, no unapproachable majesty, no repelling superiority: all was benevolence, mildness, openness, and soothing encouragement. To see, was to love; and to hear, was to trust. Timocrates shrunk from the eye of his master: it fell upon him with a fixed and deep gaze, that struck more agony into his guilty soul, than had the flash of a Cleanthes, or the glance of a Zeno. The wretch sunk beneath it: he trembled; he crouched; he looked as if he would have supplicated mercy; but his tongue cleaved to his palate, and shame withheld him from quite dropping on his knees. "Go! I will spare thee. Give way Athenians!" The scholars opened a passage: again the sage waved his hand, and the criminal slunk away.

"Your pardon, Zeno," said the Gargettian; "I know the youth: he is not worthy to stand in the portico."

"I thank you," returned the master, "and my disciples thank you. The gods forbid that we should harbor vice, or distrust virtue. I see, and I recant my error: henceforth, if I cannot respect the teacher, I shall respect the man."

"I respect both," said Epicurus, reclining his head to the stoic. "I have long known and admired Zeno: I have often mixed with the crowd in his portico, and felt the might of his eloquence. I do not expect a similar return from him, nor do I wish to allure his scholars to my gardens. I know the severity of their master, and the austerity, may I say, the intolerance of his rules. But for one," and he laid his hand upon the head of Theon, "for this one, I would bespeak clemency. Let not that be imputed to him as a crime, which has been the work of accident and of Epicurus: and let me also say for him, as well as for myself — he has lost in the gardens no virtues, if a few prejudices."

"Son of Neocles," said Zeno, "I feared you yesterday, but I fear you doubly to-day. Your doctrines are in themselves enticing, but coming from such lips, I fear they are irresistible. Methinks, I cast a prophet's eye on the map of futurity, and I see the sage of Gargettium standing on the pinnacle of fame, and a world at his feet. The world is prepared for this: the Macedonian, when he marched our legions to the conquest of Persia, struck the death-blow at Greece. Persian luxury and Persian effeminacy, which before crept, now come with strides upon us. Our youth, dandled on the lap of indulgence, shall turn with sickened ears from the severe moral of Zeno, and greedily suck in the honied philosophy of Epicurus. You will tell me that you too teach virtue. It may be so. I do not see it; but it may be so. I do not conceive how there can be two virtues, nor yet how two roads to the same. This, however, I shall not argue. I will grant that in your system, as elucidated by your practice, there may be something to admire, and much to love; but when your practice shall be dead, and your system alone shall survive, where then shall be the security of its innocence; where the antidote to its poison? Think not that men shall take the good and not the evil; soon they shall take the evil and leave the good. They shall do more; they shall pervert the very nature of the good, and make of the whole, evil unmixed. Soon, in the shelter of your bowers, all that is vicious shall find a refuge. Effeminacy shall steal in under the name of ease; sensuality and debauchery in the place of innocence and refinement; the pleasures of the body instead of those of the mind. Whatever may be your virtues, they are but the virtues of temperament, not of discipline; and such of your followers as shall be like you in temperament, may be like you in practice: but let them have boiling passions and urgent appetites, and your doctrines shall set no fence against the torrent; shall ring no alarm to the offender. Tell us not that that is right which admits of evil construction — that that is virtue which leaves an open gate to vice. I said, that with a prophet's eye I saw your future fame; but such fame as I foresee can but ill satisfy the ambition of a sage. Your gardens shall be crowded, but they shall be disgraced; your name shall be in every mouth, but every mouth shall be unworthy that speaks it; nations shall have you in honor, but ere it is so, they shall be in ruin: our degenerated country shall worship you, and expire at your feet. Zeno, meantime, may be neglected, but he shall never be slandered; the portico may be forsaken, but shall never be disgraced; its doctrines may be discarded, but shall never be misconstrued. I am not deceived by my present popularity. No school now in such repute as mine; but I know this will not last. The iron and the golden ages are run; youth and manhood are departed; and the weakness of old age steals upon the world. But, O son of Neocles! in this gloomy prospect, a proud comfort is mine: I have raised the last bulwark to the fainting virtue of man, and the departing glory of nations: — I have done more: When the virtue and glory of nations shall be dead, and when in their depraved generations some solitary souls, born for better things, shall see and mourn the vices around them, here, in the abandoned portico, shall they find a refuge; here, shutting their eyes upon the world, they shall learn to be a world to themselves; here, steeled in fortitude, shall they look down in high, unruffled majesty, on the slaves and the tyrants of the earth. Epicurus! when thou canst say this of the gardens, then, and not till then, call thyself a sage and a man of virtue." He ceased; but his full tones seemed yet to sound in the ears of his listening auditors. There was a long pause, when the Gargettian in notes like the breathing flutes of Arcadia, began his reply:

"Zeno, in his present speech, has rested much of the truth of his system on its expediency; I, therefore, shall do the same by mine. The door to my gardens is ever open, and my books are in the hands of the public; to enter, therefore, here, into the detail or the expounding of the principles of my philosophy, were equally out of place and out of season. 'Tell us not that that is right which admits of evil construction; that that is virtue which leaves an open gate to vice.' This is the thrust which Zeno now makes at Epicurus;

and did it hit, I grant it were a mortal one. From the flavour, we pronounce of the fruit; from the beauty and the fragrance, of the flower; and in a system of morals, or of philosophy, or of whatever else, what tends to produce good we pronounce to be good, what to produce evil, we pronounce to be evil. I might indeed support the argument, that our opinion with regard to the first principles of morals has nought to do with our practice; — that whether I stand my virtue upon prudence, or propriety, or justice, or benevolence, or self-love, that my virtue is still one and the same; that the dispute is not about the end, but the origin; that of all the thousands who have yielded homage to virtue, hardly one has thought of inspecting the pedestal she stands upon; that as the mariner is guided by the tides, though ignorant of their causes, so does a man obey the rules of virtue, though ignorant of the principles on which those rules are founded: and that the knowledge of those principles would affect the conduct of the man, no more than acquaintance with the causes of the tides would affect the conduct of the mariner. But this I shall not argue; in doing so I might seem but to fight you flying. I shall meet your objection in the face. And I say — that allowing the most powerful effects to spring from the first grounds of a moral system; — the worst or the best, — that mine, if the best, is to be so judged by the good it does and the evil it prevents, must be ranked among the best. If, as you say, and I partly believe, the iron and the golden ages are past, the youth and the manhood of the world, and that the weakness of old age is creeping on us — then, as you also say, our youth, dandled on the lap of indulgence, shall turn with sickened ears from the severe moral of Zeno; and then I say, that in the gardens, and in the gardens only, shall they find a food, innocent, yet adapted to their sickly palates; an armor, not of iron fortitude, but of silken persuasion, that shall resist the progress of their degeneracy, or throw a beauty even over their ruin. But, perhaps, though Zeno should allow this last effect of my philosophy to be probable, he will not approve it: his severe eye looks with scorn, not pity, on the follies and vices of the world. He would annihilate them, change them to their opposite virtues, or he would leave them to their full and natural sweep. 'Be perfect, or be as you are. I allow of no degrees of virtue, so care not for the degrees of vice.

Your ruin, if it must be, let it be in all its horrors, in all its vileness; let it attract no pity, no sympathy; let it be seen in all its naked deformity, and excite the full measure of its merited abhorrence and disgust.' Thus says the sublime Zeno, who sees only man as he should be. Thus says the mild Epicurus, who sees man as he is: — With all his weakness, all his errors, all his sins, still owning fellowship with him, still rejoicing in his welfare, and sighing over his misfortunes; I call from my gardens to the thoughtless, the headstrong, and the idle — 'Where do ye wander, and what do ye seek? Is it pleasure? Behold it here. Is it ease? Enter and repose.' Thus do I court them from the table of drunkenness and the bed of licentiousness: I gently awaken their sleeping faculties, and draw the veil from their understandings: — 'My sons! do you seek pleasure? I seek her also. Let us make the search together. You have tried wine, you have tried love; you have sought amusement in reveling, and forgetfulness in indolence. You tell me you are disappointed: that your passions grew, even while you gratified them; your weariness increased even while you slept. Let us try again. Let us quiet our passions, not by gratifying, but subduing

them; let us conquer our weariness, not by
rest, but by exertion.' Thus do I win their
ears and their confidence. Step by step I lead
them on. I lay open the mysteries of science; I
expose the beauties of art; I call the graces and
the muses to my aid; the song, the lyre, and
the dance. Temperance presides at the repast;
innocence at the festival; disgust is changed to
satisfaction; listlessness to curiosity; brutality
to elegance; lust gives place to love;
Bacchanalian hilarity to friendship. Tell me
not, Zeno, that the teacher is vicious who
washes depravity from the youthful heart;
who lays the storm of its passions, and turns
all its sensibilities to good. I grant that I do
not look to make men great, but to make men
happy. To teach them, that in the discharge of
their duties as sons, as husbands, as fathers, as
citizens, lies their pleasure and their interest;
— and when the sublime motives of Zeno
shall cease to affect an enervated generation,
the gentle persuasions of Epicurus shall still
be heard and obeyed. But you warn me that I
shall be slandered, my doctrines
misinterpreted, and my school and my name
disgraced. I doubt it not. What teacher is safe
from malevolence, what system from
misconstruction? And does Zeno really think

himself and his doctrines secure? He knows not then man's ignorance and man's folly. Some few generations, when the amiable virtues of Epicurus, and the sublime excellence of Zeno, shall live no longer in remembrance or tradition, the fierce or ambitious bigots of some new sect may alike calumniate both; proclaim the one for a libertine, and the other for a hypocrite. But I will allow that I am more open to detraction than Zeno: that while your school shall be abandoned, mine shall more probably be disgraced. But it will be the same cause that produces the two effects. It will be equally the degeneracy of man that shall cause the discarding of your doctrines, and the perversion of mine. Why then should the prospect of the future disturb Epicurus more than Zeno? The fault will not lie with me any more than you: but with the vices of my followers, and the ignorance of my judges. I follow my course, guided by what I believe to be wisdom; with the good of man at my heart, adapting my advice to his situation, his disposition, and his capacities. My efforts may be unsuccessful, my intentions maybe calumniated; but as I know these to be benevolent, so I shall continue those, unterrified and unruffled by reproaches, unchilled by occasional ingratitude and frequent disappointment." He ceased, and again laying his hand on the shoulder of Theon, led him to his master. "I ask not Zeno to admire me as a teacher, but let him not blame this scholar for loving me as a man."

"I shall not blame him," said the stoic, "but I wish that I may not soon distrust him. I wish he may not soon forget Zeno, and forsake the portico."

The shades of evening now fell on the city, and the assembly divided.

CHAPTER VIII.

The sun was in its fervor, when Theon issued
from one of the public baths. He was not
disposed for rest, yet the heat of the streets
was insufferable. "I will seek the gardens," he
thought, "and loiter in their cool shades until
the master join me." Reaching the house of
the Gargettian, and the entrance to the
gardens being shorter through it than by the
public gate, he entered, and sought the
passage he had before traversed. He however
took a wrong one, and after wandering for
some time, opened a door, and found himself
in a library. Epicurus was sitting in deep
study, with his tablets before him; his pen in
one hand, his forehead supported on the
other. Metrodorus, on the opposite side of the
room was engaged in transcribing.

Theon stopped, and, making a short apology,
hastily retired. "Stay!" cried the master. Theon
again entered, but did not advance much
within the threshold.

"When I bade you stay, I did not mean to fix
you as doorkeeper. Come in, and shut the
door behind you." Theon joyfully obeyed,

and hurried to seize the extended hand of the sage." Since you have intruded on the sanctuary, I shall not drive you out." He motioned the youth to a place on his couch. "And now, what pretty things am I to say to you for your yesterday's defense of the wicked Gargettian? You should have come home with me last night, when we were both hot from the combat, and then I could have made you an eloquent compliment in full assembly at the Symposium, and you would as eloquently have disclaimed it with one of your modest blushes."

"Then, truly, if the master had such an intention, I am very glad I did not follow him. But I passed the evening at my own lodgings, with my friend Cleanthes."

"Trying to talk him into good humor and charity, was it?"

"Something so."

"And you succeeded ?"

"Verily, I don't know; he did not leave me in worse humor than he came."

"Nay, then it must have been in better. Explanation always approaches or widens the differences between friends."

"Yes, but we also entered into argument."

"Dangerous ground that, to be sure. And your fight, of course, ended in a drawn battle."

"You pay me more than a merited compliment, in concluding that to be a thing of course."

"Nay, your pardon! I pay you any thing but a compliment. It is not that I conclude your rhetoric and your logic equal, but your obstinacy and your vanity."

"Do you know, I don't think myself either obstinate or vain," said Theon, smiling.

"Had I supposed you did, I might not have seen occasion to give you the information."

"But on what grounds do you think me obstinate and vain?"

"Your years; your years. And do you think there is a man under twenty that is not both?"

"Why, I should think an old man, at least, more obstinate than a young one."

"I grant you, when he is obstinate, which is pretty often, but not quite always; and when he is vain, the same. But whilst many old men have vanity and obstinacy in the superlative degree, all young men have those qualities in the positive. I believe your share to be tolerably moderate, but do not suppose that you have no share at all. Well, and now tell me, was it not a drawn battle?"

"I confess it was. At least, we neither of us convinced the other."

"My son, it would have added one more to the seven wonders if you had. I incline to doubt, if two men, in the course of an olympiad, enter on an argument from the honest and single desire of coming at the truth, or if, in the course of a century, one man comes from an argument convinced by his opponent."

"Well, then, if you will allow me no credit for

not being convinced, you may at least for my not being silenced, I, so young an arguer, and Cleanthes so practiced a one!"

"You broke the ice beforehand yesterday in the portico," said the philosopher, tapping his shoulder. "After that generous instance of confidence, I shall not marvel if you now find a tongue upon all proper occasions. And trust me, the breaking of the ice is a very important matter. Many an orator has made but one spring to the land, and his legs, after he had taken courage to make the first stroke. Cleanthes himself found this. You know his history? He first appeared in Athens as a wrestler, a stranger to philosophy and learning of all kinds. In our streets, however, the buzz of it could not fail to reach him. He ran full speed into the school of Crates. His curiosity, joined to his complete ignorance, gave him so singular an appearance, and produced from him so many simple questions, and blundering replies, that he received from his fellow disciples the nickname of the Ass. But the ass persevered, and soon after entering the portico, he applied with such intense diligence to the unraveling the mysteries of Zeno's philosophy, that he speedily secured the esteem of his master, and the respect of his companions. But his timidity was for some time extreme, and probably nothing but a sudden excitement could have enabled him to break through it. This, however, accidentally occurred, and he is now the ready and powerful orator that you know him."

"I have often heard," said Theon, "and really not without some skepticism, the change that a few years have wrought in Cleanthes; — *a brawny wrestler!* who could believe it: and a dull, ignorant Barbarian!"

"The world always adds marvel to the marvelous. A brawny wrestler he never was, though certainly something stouter and squarer in person than he is now; and though ignorant, he was not dull. Intense application, and, some say, the fasting of poverty, as well as temperance, rapidly reduced his body, and spiritualized his mind."

"The fasting of poverty," cried Theon, "do you believe this?"

"I fear it is possible," returned the master. "At

least it is asserted, that he possessed but four drachmas when he left the school of wrestling for that of philosophy; and it does not well appear that he now follows any other trade than that of a scholar; one which certainly brings very little nourishment to the body, whatever it may do to the mind."

"But his master; do you think Zeno would suffer him to want the necessaries of life?"

"The actual necessaries, somehow or other, he certainly has; but I can believe he will make very few serve, and procure those few with some difficulty, rather than be indebted even to his master."

"Or his friend," said Theon.

"Nay, remember, you are not a friend of very long standing, and something his junior in years."

"But should that prevent him from giving me his confidence on such an occasion?"

"Perhaps not, but allow something to the stoic pride."

"I can allow nothing to it here."

"No, because it touches your own. *Thus do I tread on the pride of Plato,*" said Diogenes, setting his foot on the robe of the academic. '*Yes, with the greater pride of Diogenes,*' returned Plato. But I have made you grave, which was not my intention. Metrodorus, how go you on?"

"Writing the last word, — There! — And now, rising and advancing towards Theon, "let me embrace the youth who so nobly took up the vindication of my insulted master. Perhaps you 'may not know how peculiarly I am indebted to you. Timocrates is the brother of Metrodorus."

"How?"

" I blush to own it."

"You need not blush, my loved son, you have done more than a brother's duty towards him, and more than a disciple's duty towards me. I suppose," turning to Theon, "as you are a stoic, you have not read the able treatises of Metrodorus in support of my doctrines, and defense of my character. In the last, indeed, he has done more than I wished."

"I own I have not, but I will read them."

"What! in the face of Zeno?"

"Aye, and of the whole portico."

"We need not doubt the young Corinthian's courage," said Metrodorus, "after his noble confidence yesterday."

"I see the master has not been silent," returned Theon, "and that he has given me more praise than is my due."

"Metrodorus can tell you that is not my custom," said the Gargettian. "By Pollux! if you continue your visits to the garden, you must look to be handled very roughly. I aim the blow at every fault I see; and I have a very acute pair of eyes. I find out the most secret sins — turn the souls of my scholars inside out; so be warned in time!"
"I do not fear you," returned the Corinthian.

"Not fear me, you rogue?"

"No, I love you too well; but," continued Theon, "let me now make my acknowledgments to the master for his coming forward so seasonably yesterday, and giving me the victory. How you astonished me! I almost took you a second time for a divinity."

"I will tell you how it happened," returned Epicurus: "Chancing to be called into the street yesterday, just after you left the house, I saw your meeting with Cleanthes; and guessing from his first address, that you would have to stand a siege, I followed you to the portico, and took my place, unnoticed, among the crowd, ready, if occasion should require, to offer my succor."

"And you heard then all that passed?"

"I did."

"I beg your pardon for the digression," said Theon: "but I think you have more forbearance and more candor than any man I ever heard of."

"If it be so, these useful qualities have not

been attained without much study and discipline; for Zeno is mistaken in thinking all my virtues the children of temperament. I very early perceived candor to be the quality the most indispensable in the composition of a philosopher, and therefore very early set my whole efforts to the attaining of it. And when once I fairly engaged in the work, I did not find it either long or difficult. I had naturally a mild temper, and a sensitive heart, and these gifts were here of inconceivable use to me. Feeling kindly towards my fellow creatures, I could the easier learn to pity rather than hate their faults; to smile, rather than frown at their follies. This was a great step gained, but the next was more difficult — to be slow in pronouncing what is a fault, and what is a folly. Our superstition would haunt with the furies the man who should take his sister to wife, while the customs of Egypt would commend them. How has the astronomer been laughed at, who made the earth revolve round the stationary sun; and yet who can say but the age may come, when this shall be established as a truth? Prejudices, when once seen as prejudices, are easily yielded. The difficulty is to come at the knowledge of them. A thousand lectures had I read to myself, ere I could calmly say, upon all occasions, it does not follow that the thing *is*, because I *think it is*; and till I could say this, I never presumed to call myself a philosopher. When I had schooled myself into candor, I found I was possessed of forbearance; for, indeed, it is hardly possible to possess the one without the other."

"I cannot understand," said Theon, "how with your mildness, your candor, and your good humor, you have so many enemies."

"Am I not the founder of a new sect?"

"Yes, but so have been many others."

"And you think I have more enemies than any? If it be so, perhaps in those peaceable qualities you have enumerated, you may seek the cause. Remember the cynics and stoics, (and I believe most of my enemies are either among them, or of their making,) do you think any of those three unpresuming virtues would secure their approbation? They do not love to see a man take the place of a philosopher, without the airs of one, and, as you may perceive, I want these most entirely.

Then you must remember also my popularity; for of course my mildness, candor, and good humor, along with other agreeable virtues which shall be nameless, help to secure me a thousand friends; and he who has many friends, must have many enemies, for you know he must be the mark of envy, jealousy, and spleen."

"I cannot endure to think that it should be so," said Theon. "Much less can I," said Metrodorus.

"My sons, never pity the man who can count more than a friend for every enemy, and I do believe that I can do this. Yes, my young stoic, Zeno may have fewer enemies, and as many disciples, but I doubt if he have so many devoted children as Epicurus."

"I know he has not," cried Metrodorus, curling his lip in proud scorn.

"You need not look so fierce upon your knowledge," said the master smiling.

"You are too mild, too candid," returned the scholar, " and that is your only fault."

"Then I am a most faultless person, and I only wish I could return the compliment to Metrodorus, but his lip curls too much, and his cheeks are too apt to kindle."

"I know it, I know it," said the scholar. "Then why not mend it?"

"Because I am not at all sure, but that it is better un-mended. If you would but turn more fiercely upon your enemies, or let me do so for you, they would respect you more, for they would fear you more."

"But as I am not a god, nor a king, nor a soldier, I have no claim to fear; and as I am a philosopher, I have no wish for it. Then, as to respect, do you really think yourself more worthy of it than your master."

"Nay," said Metrodorus, blushing, "that is too severe a rub."

"Grant that it was merited. No, no, my son, we will convince all we can, we will silence as few as possible, and we will terrify none."

"Remember the exit of Timocrates," said

Theon, "was not that made in terror?"

"Yes: but it was the work of his conscience, not of my eyes; if the first had been silent, I imagine he would have stood the last very well."

"Do not name the wretch," cried Metrodorus, indignantly. "Oh, my young Corinthian, did you know all the patience and forbearance that his master had shown towards him, all the pains he took with him, the gentleness with which he admonished him, the seriousness with which he warned him, the thousand times that he forgave him; and then, at last, when he dared to insult his master's adopted child, the lovely Hedeia, and the indignant disciples thrust him from the gardens, he goes to our enemies, the enemies of his master, and feeds their malice with infernal lies. Curses of the furies on the wretch!"

"Fie! how darest thou?" said Epicurus, thrusting his scholar indignantly from him. "Thy anger is unworthy of a man, how much then of a brother? Go, and recollect thyself, my son!" softening his voice, as he saw a tear in Metrodorus's eye. "The Corinthian will accompany you to the gardens; I will join you when I have concluded this treatise."

Metrodorus took the arm of Theon, and they left the apartment.

CHAPTER IX.

"Do not!" said Metrodorus to Theon, "take me as the best sample of the pupils of Epicurus. We are not all so hot-brained and hot-tongued."

"Nay!" returned his companion, "I am too young in philosophy to blame your warmth. In your place, I should have been as hot myself."

"I am glad to hear it. I like you the better for the sentiment. But the sun scorches dreadfully, let us seek shelter."

They turned into a thicket, and proceeding some way, caught on the still air the notes of a flute. They advanced, and came to a beautiful bank of verdure, bordered by the river, and shadowed by a group of thick and wide-spreading oaks. "It is Leontium," said Metrodorus. "No other in Attica, can breathe the flute so sweetly." They turned one of the trunks, and found her lying on the turf; her shoulder leaning against a tree, and her figure raised on one elbow. Beside her was seated the black-eyed girl whom Theon had before seen; her taper fingers twining into a wreath the scented flowers, which were lightly thrown into her lap by the gay Sofron, who stood at some distance among the shrubs.

"Enough! Enough!" said the gentle voice of the girl, as the youth shook down in showers the leaves and nectareous odors of the over-ripe blossoms. "Enough! enough! stay thy hand, thou heedless ravager!"

"Thank thee for thy words, although they chide me," said the boy, letting go the bough which he had just seized, with a bound, light as that of the shrub when it sprung upward from his hand. "Thou hast but one feeling in thy soul, Boidion; and thy nature belies the sunny clime which saw its birth. Friendship is all to thee, and that friendship is but for one."

"In truth, thou repayest his cares but coldly," said Leontium, taking the pipe from her mouth, and smiling on the dark-haired maiden.

"But I repay not thine coldly," said Boidion, kissing the hand of her friend.

"I am well punished for the neglect of my morning's lecture," said Sofron, impatiently, as he snatched his book from the ground, and turned away.

"Part not in anger, brother!" exclaimed Boidion. But the youth had vanished, and in his place Metrodorus and Theon stood before her.

The startled girl was about to rise, when Leontium, laying her hand on her arm, "Rest thee, thou timid fawn," and the maiden resumed her seat.

"I rejoice," said Theon, as he placed himself with Metrodorus by the side of Leontium, and took up the pipe which had fallen from her hand; "I rejoice to find this little instrument restored to Athens."

"Say not restored to Athens," returned Leontium, "only admitted into the garden. I doubt our vain youth still remember the curse of Alcibiades, and looking in their mirror, vow that none but fools would play on it."

"This recalls to me," said Theon, "that I have

heard among the various reports concerning the gardens current in the mouths of the Athenians, very contradictory ones as to the place allowed in it to the sciences and liberal arts, and to music in particular."

"I suppose," said Metrodorus, " that you heard our whole employment was eating, drinking, and rioting in all licentiousness."

"True, I did hear so; and I fear I must confess, half believed it. But I also heard your licentiousness described in various ways: sometimes as grossly sensual, enlivened by no elegances of art; veiled, adorned, if I may use the expression, by no refinement. In short, that Epicurus laughed as well at the fine arts as the grave sciences. From others, again, I learnt that music, dancing, poetry, and painting, were pressed into the service of his philosophy; that Leontium strung the lyre, Metrodorus the harp, Hedeia moved in the dance, Boidion raised the song to Venus; that his halls were covered with voluptuous pictures, the walks of his garden lined with indecent statues."

"And you may now perceive the truth,"

replied Metrodorus, "with your own eyes and ears."

"But," said Leontium, "the young Corinthian may be curious to know the sentiments of our master, and his advice regarding the pursuit of the sciences and the liberal arts. I can readily perceive," addressing herself to Theon, "the origin of the two contradictory reports you have just mentioned. The first you would hear from the followers of Aristippus, who, though not acknowledging the name, follow the *tenets* of his philosophy, and have long been very numerous in our degenerate city. These, because Epicurus recommends but a moderate culture of those arts, which by them are too often made the elegant incentives to licentious pleasure, accuse him of neglecting them altogether. The cynics, and other austere sects, who condemn all that ministers to the luxury, ease, or recreation of man, exaggerate his moderate use of these arts into a vicious encouragement of voluptuousness and effeminacy. You will perceive, therefore, that between the two reports lies the truth. Every innocent recreation is permitted in the garden. It is not poetry, but licentious poetry, that Epicurus condemns; not music, but voluptuous music; not painting, but licentious pictures; not dancing, but loose gestures. Yet thus he displeases alike the profligate and the austere; for these he is too moderate, and for those too severe. "With regard to the sciences, if it be said, that they are neglected among us, I do not say that our master, though himself versed in them, as in all other branches of knowledge, greatly recommends them to our study but that they are not unknown, let Polyoenus be evidence.

"He, one of the most amiable men of our school, and one most highly favored by our master, you must have heard mentioned throughout Greece as a profound geometrician."

"Yes," replied Theon, "but I have also heard, that since entering the garden, he has ceased to respect his science."

"I am not aware of that," said Leontium, "though I believe he no longer devotes to it all his time, and all his faculties. Epicurus called him from his diagrams, to open to him the secrets of physics, and the beauties of ethics; to show him the springs of human action, and lead him to the study of the human mind. He taught him, that any single study, however useful and noble in itself, was yet unworthy the entire employ of a curious and powerful intellect; that the man who pursued one line of knowledge, to the exclusion of others, though he should follow it up to its very head, would never be either learned or wise; that he who pursues knowledge, should think no branch of it unworthy attention; least of all, should he confine it to those which are unconnected with the business, and add nothing to the pleasures of life; that further not our acquaintance with ourselves, nor our fellows; that tend not to enlarge the sphere of our affections, to multiply our ideas and sensations, nor extend the scope of our inquiries. On this ground, he blamed the devotion of Polyoenus to a science that leads to other truths than those of virtue, to other study than that of man."

"I am obliged to you for the explanation," said Theon; "not because I could any longer have given credit to the absurd reports of your master's enemies; but because, whatever opens to me the character and opinions of such a man, interests and improves me."

"You will find this," said Metrodorus, " the more you consider them. The life of Epicurus is a lesson of wisdom. It is by example, even more than precept, that he guides his disciples. Without issuing commands, he rules despotically. His wishes are divined, and obeyed as laws; his opinions are repeated as oracles; his doctrines adopted as demonstrated truths. All is unanimity in the garden. We are a family of brothers, of which Epicurus is the father. And I say not this in praise of the scholars, but the master. Many of us have had bad habits, many of us evil propensities, many of us violent passions. That our habits are corrected, our propensities changed, our passions restrained, lies all with Epicurus. What I myself owe him, none but myself know. The giddy follower of licentious pleasure, the headstrong victim of my passions, he has made me taste of the sweets of innocence, and brought me into the calm of philosophy. It is thus — thus, by rendering us happy, that he lays us at his feet — thus that he gains, and holds the empire of our minds — thus that by proving himself our friend, he secures our respect, our submission, and our love. He cannot but know his power, yet he exerts it in no other way, than to mend our lives, or to keep them innocent. In argument, as you may have observed, he always seeks to convince rather than sway. He is as free from arrogance as from duplicity; he would neither force an opinion on the mind, nor conceal from it a truth. Ask his advice, and it is ever ready — his opinion, and he gives it clearly. Free from prejudice himself, he is tender to that of others; yet no fear of censure, or desire of popularity, ever leads him to humor it, either in his lessons or his writings. Candor, as you have already remarked, is the prominent feature of his mind; it is the crown of his perfect character. I say this, my young Corinthian, who know him. His soul, indeed, is open to all; but I have approached very near it, and considered its innermost recesses. Yes, I am proud to say it — I am one of those he has drawn most closely into his intimacy. With all my imperfections and errors, he has adopted me as a son; and, inferior as I am in years, wisdom and virtue, he deigns to call me his friend."

Tears here filled the eyes of the scholar; he seemed about to resume, when a slight sound made the party turn their heads, and they saw the master at their side. "Do not rise, my children, I will seat myself among you." Theon perceived he had heard the closing sentence of Metrodorus, for the water glistened in his eyes as he fixed them tenderly upon him. "Thanks, my son, for this tribute of thy gratitude; I have heard thy eulogy, and I accept it joyfully. Let all men," and he turned his eye upon Theon, "be above flattery; but let not a sage be above praise. He that is so is either arrogant or insincere. For myself, I own that the commendations of my friends fills me with triumph, as the assurance of their affection does with satisfaction. The approbation of our familiars, who are with us in our secret hours, hear our private converse, know the habits of our lives, and the bent of our dispositions, is, or should be to us, far more pleasing and triumphant than the shouts of a multitude, or the worship of the world."

There was a pause of some minutes, when Leontium took up the word. "I have been explaining, though very shortly and imperfectly, your views concerning the studies most proper to be pursued by men. I believe the Corinthian has some curiosity on this point."

Theon assented. "Knowledge," said the master, "is the best riches that man can possess. Without it, he is a brute, with it, he is a god. But like happiness, he often pursues it without finding it; or, at best, obtains of it but an imperfect glimpse. It is not that the road to it is either dark or difficult, but that he takes a wrong one; or if he enters on the right, he does so unprepared for the journey. Now he thinks knowledge one with erudition, and shutting himself up in his closet, he cons all the lore of antiquity; he fathoms the sciences, heaps up in his memory all the sayings of the dead, and reckoning the value of his acquisitions by the measure of the time and labor he hath expended on them, he is satisfied he hath reached his end, and from his retirement, looking down upon his more ignorant, because less learned, brethren, he calls them children and barbarians. But alas! Learning is not wisdom, nor will books give understanding. Again, he takes a more inviting road: he rushes into the crowd; he rolls down the stream of pleasure; he courts the breath of popularity: he unravels or weaves the riddles of intrigue ; he humors the passions of his fellows, and rises upon them to name and power. Then, laughing at the credulity, ignorance, and vice, he hath set his throne upon, he says, that to know the world is the only knowledge, and to see to dupe it, is to be wise. Yet knowledge of the world is not knowledge of man, nor to triumph in the passions of others, is not to triumph over our own. No, my sons, that only is real, is sterling knowledge, which goes to make us better and happier men, and which fits us to assist the virtue and happiness of others. All learning is useful, all the sciences are curious, all the arts are beautiful; but more useful, more curious, and more beautiful, is the perfect knowledge and perfect government of ourselves. Though a man should read the heavens, unravel their laws and their revolutions; though he should dive into the mysteries of matter, and expound the phenomena of earth and air; though he should be conversant with all the writings, and the sayings, and the actions of the dead; though he should hold the pencil of Parrhasius, the chisel of Polycletes, or the lyre of Pindar; though he should do one or all of these things, yet know not the secret springs of his own mind, the foundation of his opinions, the motives of his actions; if he hold not the rein over his passions; if he have not cleared the mist of all prejudices from his understanding; if he have not rubbed off all intolerance from his judgments; if he know not to weigh his own actions, and the actions of others, in the balance of justice — that man hath not knowledge; nor, though he be a man of science, a man of learning, or an artist, he is not a sage. He must yet sit down, patient, at the feet of philosophy. With all his learning, he hath yet to learn, and, perhaps, a harder task, he hath to unlearn."

The master here paused, but the ears of Theon still hung upon his lips. "Do not cease," he exclaimed; " I could listen to you through eternity."

"I cannot promise to declaim quite so long," returned the sage, smiling. "But if you wish it, we will follow out the topic when we have joined our other friends."

They rose, and bent their steps to the public walk.

CHAPTER X.

Epicurus stood in the midst of the expectant scholars. "My sons," he said, "why do you enter the gardens? Is it to seek happiness, or to seek virtue and knowledge? Attend, and I will show you that in finding one, you shall find the three. To be happy, we must be virtuous; and when we are virtuous, we are wise. Let us then begin: and first, let us for a while hush our passions into slumber, forget our prejudices, and cast away our vanity and our pride. Thus patient and modest, let us come to the feet of philosophy; let us say to her, 'Behold us scholars and children, gifted by nature with faculties, affections, and passions. Teach us their use and their guidance. Show us how to turn them to account — how best to make them conduce to our ease, and minister to our enjoyment.'

"Sons of earth," says the Deity, "you have spoken wisely; you feel that you are gifted by nature with faculties, affections, and passions; and you perceive that on the right exertion and direction of these depends your well-being. It does so. Your affections both of soul and body may be shortly reduced to two, pleasure and pain; the one troublesome, and the other agreeable. It is natural and befitting, therefore, that you shun pain, and desire and follow after pleasure. Set forth then on the pursuit; but ere you start, be sure that it is in the right road, and that you have your eye on the true object. Perfect pleasure, which is happiness, you will have attained when you have brought your bodies and souls into a state of satisfied tranquillity. To arrive at this, much previous exertion is requisite; yet exertion, not violent, only constant and even. And first, the body, with, its passions and appetites, demands gratification and indulgence. But beware! for here are the hidden rocks which may shipwreck your bark on its passage, and shut you out for ever from the haven of repose. Provide yourselves then with a skilled pilot, who may steer you through the Scylla and Charybdis of your carnal affections, and point the steady helm through the deep waters of your passions. Behold her! it is Prudence, the mother of the virtues, and the handmaid of wisdom. Ask, and she will tell you, that gratification will give new edge to the hunger of your appetites, and that the storm of the passions shall kindle with indulgence. Ask, and she will tell you, that sensual pleasure is pain covered with the mask of happiness. Behold she strips it from her face, and reveals the features of disease, disquietude, and remorse. Ask, and she will tell you, that happiness is not found in tumult, but tranquillity; and that, not the tranquillity of indolence and inaction, but of a healthy contentment of soul and body. Ask, and she will tell you, that a *happy life is like neither to a roaring torrent, nor a stagnant pool, but to a placid and crystal stream, that flows gently and silently along.* And now Prudence shall bring to you the lovely train of the virtues. Temperance, throwing a bridle on your desires, shall gradually subdue and annihilate those whose present indulgence would only bring future evil; and others more necessary and more innocent, she shall yet bring down to such becoming moderation, as shall prevent all disquiet to the soul and injury to the body. Fortitude shall strengthen you to bear those diseases which even temperance may not be efficient to prevent; those afflictions which fate may level at you; those persecutions which the folly or malice of man may invent. It shall fit you to bear all things, to conquer fear, and to meet death. Justice shall give you security among your fellows, and satisfaction in your own breasts.

Generosity shall endear you to others, and sweeten your own nature to yourselves. Gentleness shall take the sting from the malice of your enemies, and make you extract double sweet from the kindness of friends. Gratitude shall lighten the burden of obligation, or render it even pleasant to bear. Friendship shall put the crown on your security and your joy. With these, and yet more virtues, shall prudence surround you. And, thus attended, hold on your course in confidence, and moor your barks in the haven of repose."

"Thus says Philosophy, my sons, and says she not wisely? Tell us, ye who have tried the slippery paths of licentiousness, who have given the rein to your passions, and sought pleasure in the lap of voluptuousness; tell us, did ye find her there? No, ye did not, or ye would not now inquire of her from Epicurus. Come, then, Philosophy hath shown ye the way. Throw off your old habits, wash impurity from your hearts; take up the bridle of your passions; govern your minds, and be happy. And ye, my sons, to whom all things are yet new; whose passions yet in the bud, have never led you to pain and regret; ye who have yet to begin your career, come ye also!

Philosophy hath shown ye the way. Keep your hearts innocent, hold the bridle of your passions, govern your minds, and be happy. But, my sons, methinks I hear you say, 'You have shown us the virtues rather as modifiers and correctors of evil, than as the givers of actual and perfect good. Happiness, you tell us, consists in ease of body and mind; yet temperance cannot secure the former from disease, nor can all the virtues united award affliction from the latter.' True, my children, Philosophy cannot change the laws of nature; but she may teach us to accommodate ourselves to them. She cannot annul pain; but she can arm us to bear it. And though the evils of fate be many, are not the evils of man's coining more! Nature afflicts us with disease; but for once that it is the infliction of nature, ninety-nine times it is the consequence of our own folly. Nature levels us with death; but how mild is the death of nature, with Philosophy to spread the pillow, and friendship to take the last sigh, to the protracted agonies of debauchery, subduing the body by inches, while Philosophy is not there to give strength, nor friendship consolation, but while the flames of fever are heated by impatience, and the stings of pain envenomed by remorse! And tell me, my sons, when the body of the sage is stretched on the couch of pain, hath he not his mind to minister delight to him? Hath he not conscience whispering that his present evil is not chargeable to his own past folly, but to the laws of nature, which no effort or foresight of his could have prevented? Hath he not memory to bring to him past pleasures, the pleasures of a well-spent life, on which he may feed even while pain racks his members, and fever consumes his vitals? Or, what if agony overpower his frame, and cripple his faculties, is there not death at hand to reach him deliverance? Here, then is death, that giant of terror, acting as a friend. But does he interrupt our enjoyments as well as our sufferings? And is it for this we fear him? Ought we not rather to rejoice, seeing that the day of life has its bright and its clouded hours, that we are laid to sleep while the sun of joy yet shines, before the storm of fate has broken our tranquillity or the evening of age bedimmed our prospect? Death, then, is never our foe. When not a friend, he cannot be worse than indifferent. *For while we are, death is not; and when death is, we are not.* To be wise, then, death is nothing. Examine the ills of life; are they not of our own creation, or take they not their darkest hues from our passions or our ignorance? What is poverty, if "we have temperance, and can be satisfied with a crust, and a draught from the spring? — if we have modesty, and can wear a woolen garment as gladly as a tyrian robe? What is slander, if we have no vanity that it can wound, and no anger that it can kindle? What is neglect, if we have no ambition that it can disappoint, and no pride that it can mortify? What is persecution, if we have our own bosoms in which to retire, and a spot of earth to sit down and rest upon? What is death, when without superstition to clothe him with terrors, we can cover our heads, and go to sleep in his arms? What a list of human calamities are here expunged — poverty, slander, neglect, disappointment, persecution, death. What yet remains? Disease? That, too, we have shown temperance can often shun, and Philosophy can always alleviate. But there is yet a pain, which the wisest and the best of men cannot escape; that all of us, my sons, have felt, or have to feel. Do not your hearts whisper it? Do you not tell me, that in death there is yet a sting? That ere he aim at us, he may level the beloved of our soul? The father, whose tender care hath reared our infant minds — the brother, whom the same breast hath nourished, and the same roof sheltered, with whom, side by side, we have grown like two plants by a river, sucking life from the same fountain and strength from the same sun — the child whose gay prattle delights our ears, or whose opening understanding fixes our hopes — the friend of our choice, with whom we have exchanged hearts, and shared all our pains and pleasures, whose eye hath reflected the tear of sympathy, whose hand hath smoothed the couch of sickness. Ah! my sons, here indeed is a pain — a pain that cuts into the soul. There are masters that will tell you otherwise; who will tell you that it is unworthy of a man to mourn even here. But such, my sons, speak not the truth of experience or philosophy, but the subtleties of sophistry and pride. He who feels not the loss, hath never felt the possession. He who knows not the grief, hath never known the joy. See the price of a friend in the duties we render him, and the sacrifices we make to him, and which, in making, we count not sacrifices, but pleasures. We sorrow for his sorrow; we supply his wants, or, if we cannot, we share them. We follow him to exile. We close ourselves in his prison; we soothe him in sickness; we strengthen him in death: nay, if it be possible, we throw down our life for his. Oh! What a treasure is that for which we do so much! And is it forbidden to us to mourn its loss? If it be, the power is not with us to obey. Should we, then, to avoid the evil, forego the good? Shall we shut love from our hearts, that we may not feel the pain of his departure? No; happiness forbids it. Experience forbids it. Let him who hath laid on the pyre the dearest of his soul, who hath washed the urn with the bitterest tears of grief — let him say if his heart hath ever formed the wish that it had never shrined within it him whom he now deplores. Let him say if the pleasures of the sweet communion of his former days doth not still live in his remembrance. If he love not to recall the image of the departed, the tones of his voice, the words of his discourse, the deeds of his kindness, the amiable virtues of his life. If, while he weeps the loss of his friend, he smiles not to think that he once possessed him. He who knows not friendship, knows not the purest pleasure of earth. Yet if fate deprive us of it, though we grieve, we do not sink; Philosophy is still at hand, and she

upholds us with fortitude. And think, my
sons, perhaps in the very evil we dread, there
is a good; perhaps the very uncertainty of the
tenure gives it value in our eyes; perhaps all
our pleasures take their zest from the known
possibility of their interruption. What were
the glories of the sun, if we knew not the
gloom of darkness? What the refreshing
breezes of morning and evening, if we felt not
the fervors of noon? Should we value the
lovely-flower, if it bloomed eternally; or the
luscious fruit, if it hung always on the bough?
Are not the smiles of the heavens more
beautiful in contrast with their frowns, and
the delights of the seasons more grateful from
their vicissitudes? Let us then be slow to
blame nature, for perhaps in her apparent
errors there is hidden a wisdom. Let us not
quarrel with fate, for perhaps in our evils lie
the seeds of our good. Were our body never
subject to sickness, we might be insensible to
the joy of health. Were our life eternal, our
tranquillity might sink into inaction. Were
our friendship not threatened with
interruption, it might want much of its
tenderness. This, then, my sons, is our duty,
for this is our interest and our happiness; to
seek our pleasures from the hands of the

virtues, and for the pain which may befall us, to submit to it with patience, or bear up against it with fortitude. *To walk, in short, through life innocently and tranquilly; and to look on death as its gentle termination, which it becomes us to meet with ready minds, neither regretting the past, nor anxious for the future."*

The sage had scarcely ceased, when a scholar advanced from the crowd, and bowing his head with reverence, stooped and touched the knees of his master. "Refuse not my homage," he said, "nor call the expression of it presumptuous." Epicurus raised him in his arms. "Colotes, I am more proud of the homage of thy young mind, than I should be of that of the assembled crowds of Olympia. May thy master, my son, never lose his power over it, as I feel that he will never abuse it."

CHAPTER XI.

The sun had far declined from his meridian, yet no cool breeze tempered the fervors of the heat. The air was chained in oppressive stillness, when suddenly a bustling wind shook the trees, and a low growling reverberated round the horizon. The scholars retired before the threatening storm; but Theon, his ear still filled with the musical voice of the sage, and his heart imbued with his gentle precepts, lingered to feed alone upon the thoughts they had awakened in him. "How mad is the folly of man," he said, as he threw his back against a tree. "Professing to admire wisdom and love virtue, and yet ever persecuting and slandering both. How vain is it to look for credit by teaching truth, or to seek fame by the road of virtue!"

"Thy regret is idle, my son," said a well known voice in his ear.

"Oh! my guardian spirit!" cried the startled youth — "Is it you ?"

"I linger," said the Gargettian, "to watch the approach of the storm, and I suppose you do the same."

"No," returned the youth; "I hardly heeded the heavens."

"They are singular, however, at this moment." Theon looked where the sage pointed; a dark mass of vapors was piled upon the head of Hymettus, from which two columns, shooting forth like the branches of some giant oak, spread themselves over the sky. The opposing sun, fast traveling to the horizon, looked red through the heated atmosphere, and flashed a deep glare on their murky sides. Soon half the landscape was blackened with the sinking clouds, that each moment increasing in bulk and density, seemed to touch the bosom of the earth. The western half glowed with a brilliant light, like molten gold. The distant outline was marked with a pencil of fire, while the gardens and villas that speckled the plain, seemed illuminated in jubilee.

"See," said the sage, stretching his hand towards the gilded scene; "see the image of that fame which is not founded in virtue. Thus bright may it shine for a moment, but the cloud of oblivion or infamy comes fast to cover its glory."

"Is it so?" said Theon. "Do not the vile of the
earth fill the tongues of men, and are not the
noble forgotten? Does not the titled murderer
inscribe his name on the tablets of eternity,
with the sword which is dipped in the blood
of his fellows? And does not the man who has
spent his youth, and manhood, and age, in the
courts of wisdom — who has planted peace at
the hearth, and given truth to the rising age,
does he not go down to the grave in silence,
his bones unhonored, and his name
forgotten?"
"Possibly his name; but, if he have planted
peace at the hearth, and given truth to the
rising age, surely not his better part — his
virtues. Do not confound noise with fame.
The man who is remembered, is not always
honored; and reflect, what a man toils for, that
probably will he win. The titled murderer,
who weaves his fate with that of empires, will
with them go down to posterity. The sage,
who does his work in the silence of
retirement, unobserved in his own generation,
will pass into the silence of the grave,
unknown to the future."

"But suppose he be known. How few worshipers should crowd to his shrine, and what millions to that of the other!"

"And those few, my son, who are they? The wise of the earth, the enlightened patriot, the discerning philosopher. And who are the millions? The ignorant, the prejudiced, and the idle. Nor yet, let us so wrong the reason of our species, as to say, that they always give honor to the mischievous rather than the useful — gratitude to their oppressors, rather than their benefactor. In instances they may be blind, but in the gross they are just. The splendor of action, the daring of enterprise, or the glitter of majesty, may seize their imagination, and so drown their judgment; but never is it the tyranny of power, the wantonness of cruelty, the brutality of vice, which they adore, any more than it is the innocence and usefulness of virtue, which they despise. The united experience of mankind has pronounced virtue to be the great good: nay, so universal is the conviction, that even those who insult her in their practice, bow to her in their understanding. Man is for the most part more fool than knave, more weak than depraved in action, more ignorant than vicious in judgment; and seldom is he so weak and so ignorant, as not to see his own interest, and value him who promotes it. But say that he often slanders the virtuous, and persecutes the wise; he does it more in error than from depravity. He is credulous, and on the report of malice, takes virtue for hypocrisy; — he is superstitious, and some of the truths of wisdom appear to him profane. Say he does homage to vice — you will find when he does it, he believes her to be virtue. Hypocrisy has masked her deformity, or talent decked her with beauty. Is here, then, subject for wrath? Rather, surely, for compassion. Is here matter for disgust? Rather, surely, for exertion. The darker the ignorance, the more praise to the sage who dispels it; — the deeper the prejudice, more fame to the courage which braves it. But may the courage be vain? May the sage fall the victim of the ignorance he combats? He may; he often has. But ere he engage, knows he not the risk? The risk is to himself; the profit to mankind. To a benevolent soul, the odds is worth the throw; and though it be against him at the present, he may win it in the future. The sage, whose vision is cleared from the mists of prejudice, can stretch it over the existing age, to the kindling horizon of the succeeding, and see, perhaps, unborn generations weeping the injustice of their fathers, and worshiping those truths which they condemned. Or is it otherwise? Lives he in the old age of the world, and does he see the stream of time flowing through a soil yet more rank with prejudice and evil? Say then — were the praise of such a world a fit object of his ambition, or shall he be jealous of the fame which ignorance yields to the unworthy? But any way, my son, it is not the voice of fame that we should seek in the practice of virtue, but the peace of self-satisfaction. The object of the sage is to make himself independent of all that he cannot command within himself. Yet, when I speak of independence, I mean not indifference; while we make ourselves sufficient for ourselves, we need not forget the crowd about us. We are not wise in the contempt of others but in calm approbation of ourselves."

"Still dost thou droop thy head, my son?" said the gentle philosopher, laying a hand on the shoulder of his young friend.

"Your words sink deep into my soul," replied Theon; "yet they have not chased the melancholy they found there. I have not such a world in myself as to be independent of that about me, nor can I forgive the offenses of my fellows, merely because they commit them from ignorance. Nay, is not their very ignorance often a crime, when the voice of truth is whispering in their ear?"

"And if they do not hear her whisper in the one ear, it is because prejudice is crying aloud into the other."

"Prejudice! I hate prejudice," said Theon.

"And so do I," said the master.

"Yes, but I am provoked with it."

"I suspect that will not remove the evil."

"Nothing will remove it. It is inherent in men's nature."

"Then as we are men, it may be inherent in ours. Trust me, my son, it is better to correct ourselves, than to find fault with our neighbors."

"But is it not allowed to do both? Can we help seeing the errors of the world in which we live, and seeing, can we help being angry at them?"

"Certainly not the seeing them, but I hope, very possibly, the being angry with them. He that loses temper with the folly of others, shows that he has folly himself. In which case they have as much right to complain of his, as he of theirs. And have I not been trying to show you, that when you are wise you will be independent of all that you cannot command within yourself? You say you are not so now. I admit it, but when you are wise you will be so. And *till* you are wise, you have surely no title to quarrel with another's ignorance."

"I can never be independent of my friends," returned Theon. "I must ever feel the injustice done to them though I might be regardless of that which affected merely myself."

"Why so? What would enable you to disregard that done to yourself?"

"Conscious innocence. Pride, if you will. Contempt of the folly and ignorance of my judges."

"Well, and are you less conscious of the innocence of your friend? If you are, where is your indignation? And if you are not, have you less pride for him than for yourself? Do you respect that folly and ignorance in his judges, that you despise in your own?"

"I believe it will not stand argument," said Theon. "But you must forgive me if, when I contemplate Epicurus, I feel indignant at the slander which dares to breathe upon his purity."

"And do you think you were yourself an object of indignation, when you spoke of him as a monster of vice ?"

"Yes, I feel I was."

"But he felt otherwise," said the master, "and which, think you, is likely to feel most wisely?"

"Ah! I hope it is Epicurus," said the youth,

snatching his instructor's hand. This conversation was here interrupted by the bursting of the storm. The fire flashed round the horizon, the thunder cracked over the zenith, and the first big drops fell from the burdened clouds. "We are near the Temple," said the sage, "let us seek shelter under its portico. We may watch the storm there, without a wet skin." They had hardly gained it, when the rain poured down in torrents. Ilisus, whom the burning sun had of late faded into a feeble rill, soon filled and overflowed his bed; wave after wave, in sudden swell, came roaring down, as if he now first burst to life from the womb of his parent mountain. But the violence of the storm soon spent its strength. Already the thunder broke with longer intervals, and a faint light, like the opening of morning, gleamed over the western heavens. At length the sun cleared his barrier of clouds. He stood on the verge of the waves, and shot his level rays over the blazing Salamis and the glistening earth. The sage stood with his young friend in silent admiration, when the eye of the latter was attracted by a horseman, who came full gallop over the plain, directly towards them. The object of his attention had nearly reached the river, when he perceived the rider to be a female. The swift feet of the steed now touched the opposing bank. "Great Jove, he will not attempt the passage," exclaimed the youth, as he sprung towards the river. "Stop, stop," he cried. She checked the rein, but too late. The animal, accustomed to the passage, and blinded by speed, plunged into the flood. Theon tore his robe from his shoulders, and was about to make the plunge on his side, when he was grasped by Epicurus.

"Be not rash. The horse is strong, and the rider skillful." The voice that uttered these words was calm and distinct, but its wonted music was changed into the deep tone of suppressed horror. Even at that moment, the accent struck Theon's ear.

"Do you know her? Is she your friend? Is she dear to you? If so" — he made another effort to throw himself forward, but was still restrained by Epicurus. He looked into the philosopher's face. There was no motion in it, save a quivering round the mouth, while the eyes were fixed in aching gaze on the struggling animal. He breasted the water midway, when seemingly frightened at the rapidity of the current, he tried to turn. The rider saw the danger, she curbed the rein, she tried with voice and effort to urge him to the conflict. Theon looked again at the sage. He saw he had loosened his mantle, and was prepared to try the flood. "I conjure you, by the gods!" said the youth, "what is my life to yours?" He grasped the sage in his turn. "Let me save her! I will save her — I swear it." They both struggled a moment for the leap. "I swear," continued Theon, with furious energy, "that if you go I will follow." He made another effort, and dashed from the hold of Epicurus into the river. Naturally strong, he was doubly so at this moment. He felt not fear, he saw not danger. In a moment he was in the centre of the current — another stroke, and he had seized the mane of the steed. But the terrified animal even then gave way to the stream. The rider still struggled for her seat. But her strength fast failed, she stretched out her hand with a feeble cry of despair. Theon shot forward yet swifter than the tide; he drove with a shock against the horse, and caught with one arm the expiring girl. Then, half yielding to the current, he parted with the other the roaring waters, and with effort almost superhuman, grappled with their fury. Panting, choking, bewildered, yet never relaxing, he reached, but he knew not how, the land. When he recovered recollection, he found himself lying on a couch, in the arms of Epicurus. "Where am I," he said, "and where is the lovely girl?"

"Safe, safe, as her generous deliverer. Oh, my son! now indeed my son, when I owe to thee my Hedeia."

"Was it your adopted child, then," cried the youth, with a shout of delirious joy, as he threw himself on the breast of the sage. "But tell me," he said, rising and looking round on Metrodorus, who, with two other scholars, stood beside the couch, "how came I here?"

"I believe," said Metrodorus, "the master swam to your aid — at least we found him lifting you and Hedeia from the water."

"I watched your strength, my son, and reserved mine till it should fail; when I observed it do so, I came to your assistance. Now, compose yourself awhile, and I will go and put myself into a dry tunic."

CHAPTER XII.

Theon, rising, recruited from the warm bath, and his limbs being well rubbed with ointments, joined the party at supper in health and spirits. It consisted of the master, Leontium, Metrodorus, and two other scholars, whose persons were new to him. There was something in the gentle manners of one, not unmixed with a little awkwardness, the grave repose of his features, the abstract thought that lined his forehead, and fixed his mild eye, that led him to guess it was Polyoenus. The other, whose gait had the dignity of manhood, and the polish of art; whose face, without being handsome, had that beauty which refined sentiment and a well stored mind always throw more or less into the features; whose whole appearance showed at once the fine scholar and the amiable man, fixed instantly Theon's attention and curiosity. All received the youth with congratulations, and Metrodorus, as he held him in his embrace, jokingly upbraided him as a greedy and barbarous invader, who was carrying off, in his single person, the whole love and honor of the garden. "But yet," he added, "have a care; for I doubt you have secured the envy also."

"I believe it," said Theon. "At least I know I should envy you, or any of your fraternity, who had risked his life, aye, or lost it, in service of your master, or any your master loved."

"Well said, my dear youth," said the stranger, taking his hand; "and when you have seen more of the nymph you so gallantly rescued, you will perhaps think the man a no less object of envy, who should risk his life for her, or any he loved."

They moved to the table, when Leontium whispered Theon, "Hermarchus of Mytelene, the bosom friend of Epicurus."

"I thank you," replied Theon, "you have well read my curiosity."

The party were about to place themselves when a sound in the passage turned all eyes to the door. "Yes, nurse, you may just peaceably let me take my own way. Go, go, I am quite well, quite warm, and quite active. I tell you, you have rubbed my skin off" —

would you rub away my flesh too?" And in came, with the light foot of a nymph of Dian, the young Hedeia. A white garment, carelessly adjusted, fell with inimitable grace, over her airy form; in equal negligence, her long hair, still moist from the recent waves, and disheveled by the anxious rubbing of her careful attendant, hung down her shoulders to her zone. Her face, though pale from late alarm and fatigue, beaming with life and joy. Her full dark eyes sparkling with intelligence, and her lips, though their coral was slightly faded, lovely with smiles. In one hand she held a goblet, in the other a chaplet of myrtle. "Which is my hero?" she asked in a voice more sweet than the evening zephyr, as she looked round the board - "Am I right?" approaching Theon. The youth, as he gazed on the lovely face, forgot to answer. "Nay, is it a statue?" leaning forward, and gazing in her turn, as if in curious inspection.

"No, a slave," said Theon, half smiling, half blushing, as he stooped his knee, while she placed the garland on his head. "I come to pledge you," she said, putting the cup to her lips, "and to bid you pledge me," presenting it with bewitching grace to the youth. He took it in speechless ecstasy from her taper fingers, and turning that side to his mouth which had received the touch of hers, quaffed at once the draught of wine and love."

"Beware," said a voice in his ear: "it is the cup of Circe." He turned, Polyoenus stood behind him; but when he saw his motionless features, he could hardly believe the whisper had been uttered by him.

"I know," continued the fair one, pointing to the table, "there is but cold beverage here for a drowned man. My wise father may know to give comfort to the mind, but come to my good nurse, when you want the comfort of the body. She is the most skillful compounder of elixirs, philters, and every palatable medicine, that you might haply find in all Greece, all Asia, aye, or all the earth. And now make way," putting back the surrounding company, and leading Theon by the arm to the upper end of the table. "Behold the king of the feast."

"That is, if you are the queen," said the intoxicated youth.

"Oh, certainly," placing herself by his side, " I

never refuse consequence, whenever I can get it."

"Whenever you can take it, you mean," said the master, laughing.

"And is not that everywhere?" said Hermarchus, bowing to the fair girl.

"Yes, I believe it is. A pretty face, my friends, may presume much; a wilful nature may carry all things. I have both to perfection; have I not?"

"Praise to Venus, and the Graces," said Leontium; "our sister has brought a heart as gay from the college of Pythagoras, as she took into it."

"To be sure; and did you expect otherwise? Psha! you philosophers know nothing of human nature. I could have told you before this last experiment, that humor lies in contrast, and that a wag will find more subject in a synod of grave sages than a crew of laughing wits. You must know," turning to Theon, "I have been on a visit to a wise man, a very wise man, who has followed from his youth up the whim, and all very wise men have whims, of restoring the neglected school of Pythagoras to its pristine greatness. Accordingly, he has collected and brought up some dozen submissive youths to his full satisfaction; for not one of them dare know his right hand from his left, but on his master's authority, doubly backed by that of the great founder. They have, in short, no purse of their own, no time of their own, no tongue of their own, no will of their own, and no thought of their own. You cannot conceive a more perfect community. One more virtuously insipid, more scientifically absurd, or more wisely ignorant."

"Fie, fie you giddy girl," said the master, smiling, while he tried to frown.

"Giddy, not at all. I am delivering a grave matter of fact story."

"And we are all here," said Hermarchus, "so pray let us have the whole of it."

"The whole? nay, you have it already. An abode of the blessed; a house with twelve bodies in it, and one brain to serve them all."

"Why," replied Hermarchus, " I believe you have at home some hundred bodies in the same predicament."

"To be sure; and so I told the sage Pythagorean, when he looked so complacently on his eleven pieces of mechanism, and assured him that were it not for me, there would not be a single original in the garden, save the master. I assure you, father, I gave just as matter of fact a description of your household, as I now do of the old Pythagorean's. And, a most singular coincidence, I remember he cried, 'Fie, fie,' just as you did now. Once more, it was a most perfect household; with the men, all peace, method, virtue, learning and absurdity; with the women, all silence, order, ignorance, modesty, and stupidity."

"And pray, sister," said Metrodorus, "what made you leave a society that afforded such rich food to your satire?"

"Because, brother, the richest food cloys the fastest. I passed three days to my perfect satisfaction; a fourth would have killed me."

"And your friends too," said the philosopher, shaking his head.

"Killed them. They never knew they had life, till I found it out for them. No, no, I left sore hearts behind me. The master indeed — ah, the master! poor man, shall I confess it? Before I left the house, he caught one of his pupils looking into a mirror with a candle, heard that another had stirred the fire with a sword, and oh! more dreadful than all, that a third had swallowed a bean. If I could but have stayed three days longer, I might have wound my girdle round the necks of the whole dozen, brought them on my back, and laid them at the feet of Epicurus."

"And what said the master, all this time?" said Leontium.

"Said he? what said he? umph! I never heard what he said, for I was reading what he felt."

"And what felt he?" asked Hermarchus.

"Just what *you* have felt — and you too," looking at Polyoenus. "Aye, and you also, very sage philosopher;" and turning short round to Theon, "what you have to feel, if you have not yet felt — that I was vastly witty, vastly amusing, and vastly beautiful."

"And do you think," said the Gargettian, "when we feel all this, we can't be angry with you?"

"Nay, what do *you* think? But no, no, I know you all better than you know yourselves. And I think you *cannot*, or if you *can*, 'tis as the poet, who curses the muse he burns to propitiate. Oh philosophy! philosophy! thou usest hard maxims and showest a grave face, yet thy maxims are but words, and thy face but a mask. A skillful histrion, who, when the buskin is off, paint, plaster, and garment thrown aside, stands no higher, no fairer, and no more mighty, than the youngest, poorest, and simplest of thy gaping worshipers. Ah, friends! laugh and frown; but show me the man, the wisest, the gravest, or the sourest, that a bright pair of eyes can't make a fool of."

"Ah, you proud girl," said Hermarchus, "tremble! remember, the blue-eyed Sappho died at last for a Phaon."

"Well, if such be my fate, I must submit. I do not deny, because I have been wise hitherto, that I may not turn fool with the philosophers before I die."

"What an excellent school for the rearing of youth," said the master, "the old Pythagorean must think mine."

"Judging from me as a specimen, you mean. And trust me now, father, I am the best. Do I not practice what you preach? What you show the way to, do I not possess? Look at my light foot, look in my laughing eye, read my gay heart, and tell — if pleasure be not mine. Confess, then, that I take a shorter cut to the goal than your wiser scholars, aye than your wisest self. You study, you lecture, you argue, you exhort. And what is it all for? as if you could not be good without so much learning, and happy without so much talking. Here am I — I think I am very good, and I am quite sure I am very happy; yet I never wrote a treatise in my life, and can hardly listen to one without a yawn."

"Theon," said Epicurus, smiling, "you see now the priestess of our midnight orgies."

"Ah! poor youth, you must have found the garden but a dull place in my absence. But have patience, it will be better in future."

"More dangerous," said Polyoenus.

"Never mind him," whispered Hedeia, in the Corinthian's ear — "he is not the grave man that a bright pair of eyes cannot make a fool of. This is very odd," she continued, looking round the board. "Here am I, the stranger, and one too half drowned, charged with the entertaining of this whole learned society."

"Nay, my girl," said the master, "thou hadst need to be whole drowned, ere your friends might secure the happiness of being listened to."

"Indeed, I believe it's true; and considering that the greatest pleasure of life is the being listened to, I wonder how any one was found to pick me out of the water. The Corinthian, to be sure, did not know what he saved; but that the master should wet his tunic in my service is a very unaccountable circumstance. Is there any reason for it in philosophy?"

"I am afraid none."

"Or in mathematics?" turning to Polyoenus. "Now, just see there a proof of my argument. Can any man look more like wisdom, or less like happiness? This comes of diagrams and ethics. My young Corinthian, take warning."

"I wish we could fix you to a diagram," said Leontium.

"The Graces forfend! and why should you wish it? Think you it would make me wiser? Let Polyoenus be judge, if I am not wiser than he. I admire the different prescriptions that are given by different doctors. The wife of the good Pythagorean recommended me a distaff."

"Well," said Hermarchus, "that might do equally."

"Pray, why don't you take one yourself?"

"I, you see, am busy with philosophy."

"And so am I, with laughing at it. Ah, my sage brother, every man thinks *that* perfection, that he is himself — *that* the only knowledge that he possesses — and *that* the only pleasure that he pursues. Trust me, there are as many ways of living as there are men, and one is no more fit to lead another, than a bird to lead a fish, or a fish a quadruped."

"You would make a strange world, were you the queen of it," said Hermarchus, laughing.

"Just as strange, and no stranger, than it is at present. For why? I should take it as I found it, and leave it as I found it. 'Tis your philosophers, who would rub and twist, and plague and doctor it, and fret your souls out, to bring all its heterogeneous parts, fools, wits, knaves, simpletons, grave, gay, light, heavy, long-faced, and short-faced, black, white, brown, straight and crooked, tall, short, thin and fat, to fit together, and patiently reflect each other, like the acorns of an oak, or the modest wives and helpless daughters of the good citizens of Athens; 'tis you, I say, who would make a strange world, were you kings of it — you who would shorten and lengthen, clip, pull, and carve men's minds to fit your systems, as the tyrant did men's bodies to fit his bed."

"I grant there's some truth, my girl, in thy nonsense," said the master.

"And I grant that there is not a philosopher in Athens, who would have granted as much, save thyself. You will find my young hero," turning to Theon, that my father philosophizes more sense, that is, less absurdity, than any man since the seven sages; nay! even than the seven sages philosophized themselves. He only lacks to be a perfectly wise man --"

"To burn," said the master, "his books of philosophy, and to sing a tune to thy lyre."

"No, it shall do to let me sing a tune to it myself." She bounded from the couch and the room, and returned in a moment, with the instrument in her hand. "Fear not," she said, nodding to the sage, as she lightly swept the chords, " I shall not woo my own lover, but your mistress."

Come, Goddess! Come! not in thy power,
With gait and garb austere,
And threatning brow severe,
Like stern Olympus in the judgment hour;
But come with looks the heart assuring.

Come with smiling eyes alluring.
Moving soft to Lydian measures,
Girt with graces, loves, and pleasures.
Bound with Bazilea's zone.
Come, Virtue; come! in joyous tone
We bid thee welcome to our hearth,
For well we know that thou alone
Canst give the purest bliss of earth."

"No thanks, no thanks. I shall take my own reward," and stealing behind Epicurus, she threw her white arms around his neck, and laid her cheek on his lips. Then rising, "Good dreams be with you," and waving round her hand, and throwing a smile on Theon, vanished in an instant. The youth saw and heard no more, but sat as in a dream, until the party divided.

"Have a care," whispered the master, as he followed him into the vestibule. "Cupid is a knavish god; he can pierce the hearts of others, and hold a shield before his own."

CHAPTER XIII.

Night's refreshing airs fanned the cheeks of Theon, and rustled the myrtle on his brow; but the subtle fever of love which swept through his veins, and throbbed in his heart and temples, was beyond their cooling influence. The noisy business of life had now given place in the streets to noisy merriment. The song and the dance sounded from the open portals; and the young votaries of Bacchus, in all the frenzy of the god, rushed from the evening banquet, to the haunts of midnight excess, while the trembling lover glided past to the stolen interview, shrinking even from the light of Day's pale sister. Theon turned abruptly from the crowd, and sought instinctively a public walk, at this hour always private, where he had often mused on the mysteries of philosophy, and taxed his immature judgment to hold the balance between the doctrines of her contending schools. No thoughts so deep and high now filled his youthful fancy. He wandered on, his senses steeped in delirium not less potent than that of wine, until his steps were suddenly arrested by a somewhat rude encounter with a human figure, advancing with a pace more deliberate than his own. He started backwards and his eyes met those of Cleanthes. The stoic paused a moment, then moved to pass on. But Theon, however little he might have desired such a companion at such a moment, hailed him by name, and placed himself at his side. Again Cleanthes gazed on him in silence; when Theon, following the direction of his glance, raised a hand to his temples, and removed, with a conscious blush, the offending garland. He held it for a moment; then, placing it in his bosom — "You misjudge this innocent token; — a pledge of acknowledgment for a life redeemed from the waves."

"Would that I might receive a pledge of the redemption of thy virtue, Theon, from the flood of destruction! For thy sake I have opened the volumes of this smooth deceiver. And shall a few fair words and a fairer countenance shield such doctrines from opprobrium? Shall he who robs virtue of her sublimity, the gods of their power, man of his immortality, and creation of its providence, pass for a teacher of truth, and expounder of the laws of nature? Where is thy reason, Theon? where thy moral sense? to see, in doctrines such as these, aught but impiety and crime, or to imagine, that he, who advocates them, can merit aught but the scorn of the wise, and the opprobrium of the good?"

"I know not such to be the doctrines of Epicurus," said the youth, "and you will excuse my farther reply, until I shall have examined the philosophy you so bitterly, and apparently so justly condemn."

"The philosophy? honor it not with the name."

"Nay," returned Theon with a smile, "There are so many absurdities honored with that appellative, in Athens, that the compliment might pass unchallenged, although applied to one less worthy than, in my eyes, appears the sage of Gargettium. But," preventing the angry interruption of the stoic, "my slowness to judge and to censure offends your enthusiasm. The experience of three days has taught me this caution. My acquaintance, as yet, is rather with the philosopher than the philosophy; my prejudices at first were equally strong against both. Having discovered my error with respect to one, ought I not to read, listen, and examine, before I condemn the other. And, the rather, as all that I have heard in the garden has hitherto convinced my reason, and awakened my admiration and love."

"Permit me the question," said Cleanthes, stopping short, and fixing his piercing glance on the countenance of his companion — "Honor ye the Gods, and believe ye in a creating cause, and a superintending Providence?"

"Surely I do," said Theon.

"How, then, venerate ye the man who proclaims his doubt of both?"

"So, in my hearing, has never the son of Neocles."

"But he has and does in the hearing of the world."

"I have so heard, and ranked it among the libels of his enemies."

"He has so written, and the fact is acknowledged by his friends."

"I will read his works," said Theon, "and question the writer. A mind more candid, whatever be its errors, exists not, I am persuaded, than that of Epicurus; I should have said also, a mind more free of errors. But he has taught me to think no mind, however wise, infallible."

"Call ye such doctrines, errors? I should rather term them crimes."

"I object not to the word," said Theon. "'I will examine into this. The Gods have ye in their keeping! Good night." They entered the city, and the friends divided.

CHAPTER XIV.

Uneasy thoughts bred unquiet slumbers; and Theon rose from a restless couch, before the first blush of Aurora tinged the forehead of the sky. He trod the paths of the garden, and waited with impatience, for the first time not unmixed with apprehension, the appearance of the Master. The assertions of Cleanthes were corroborated by the testimony of the public; but that testimony he had learned to despise. They were made after perusal of Epicurus' writings; with these writings he was still unacquainted. Had they been misinterpreted? Cleanthes was no Timocrates. If prejudiced, he was incapable of wilful misrepresentation; and he was too familiar with the science of philosophy, so grossly to misunderstand a reasoner, as lucid as appeared to be Epicurus. These musings were soon interrupted. The morning star still glowed in the kindling east, when he heard approaching footsteps, and turning from the shades upon a small open lawn where a crystal fountain flowed from the inverted urn of a recumbent naiad, he was greeted by the Sage.

"Oh no," exclaimed Theon half audibly, as he gazed on the serene countenance before him, "this man is not an Atheist."

"What thoughts are with you, my Son, this morning?" said the philosopher, with kind solicitude. "I doubt your plunge in Ilyssus disturbed your dreams. Did the image of a fair nymph, or of a river God flit round your couch, and drive sleep from your eyelids?"

"I was in some danger from the first," said the youth, half smiling, half blushing, "until a visitant of a different character, and one, I imagine, more wont to soothe than to disturb the mind, brought to my imagination a host of doubts and fears, which your presence alone has dispelled."

"And who played the part of your Incubus?" demanded the Sage.

"Even yourself, most benign and indulgent of men."

"Truly, I grieve to have acted so ill by thee, my Son. It shall be well, however, if having inflicted the disease, I may be its physician."

"On leaving you, last night," said Theon, "I encountered Cleanthes. He came from the perusal of your writings, and brought charges against them which I was unprepared to answer."

"Let us hear them, my Son; perhaps, until you shall have perused them yourself, we may assist your difficulty."

"First, that they deny the existence of the gods."

"I see but one other assertion that could equal that in folly," said Epicurus.

"I knew it," exclaimed Theon, triumphantly; "I knew it was impossible. But where will not prejudice lead men, when even the upright Cleanthes is capable of slander!"

"He is utterly incapable of it," said the Master ; "and the inaccuracy, in this case, I rather suspect to rest with you than with him. To *deny* the existence of the gods would indeed be presumption in a philosopher; a presumption equaled only by that of him who should *assert* their existence."

"How!" exclaimed the youth, with a countenance in which astonishment seemed to suspend every other expression.

"As I never saw the gods, my son," calmly continued the Sage, "I cannot *assert* their existence; and, that I never saw them, is no reason for my *denying* it."

"But do we believe nothing except that of which we have ocular demonstration?"

"Nothing, at least, for which we have not the evidence of one or more of our senses; that is, when we believe on just grounds, which, I grant, taking men collectively, is very seldom."

"But where would this spirit lead us? To impiety! — to Atheism! — to all, against which I felt confidence in defending the character and philosophy of Epicurus!"
"We will examine presently, my Son, into the meaning of the terms you have employed. But as respects your defense of my philosophy, I am sorry that you presumed so much, where you knew so little. Let this serve for another caution against pronouncing

before you examine, and asserting before you inquire. It is my usual custom," continued the Master, "with the youth who frequent my school, to defer the discussion of all important questions until they are naturally, in the course of events, suggested to their own minds. Their curiosity once excited, it is my endeavor, so far as in me lies, to satisfy it. When you first entered the garden your mind was unfit for the examination of the subject you have now started: it is no longer so; and we will therefore enter upon the inquiry, and pursue it in order."

"Forgive me if I express — if I acknowledge," said the youth, slightly recoiling from his instructor, "some reluctance to enter on the discussion of truths, whose very discussion would seem to argue a doubt, — and - "

"And what then?"

"That very doubt were a crime."

"It is there that I wished to lead you; and with the examination of this point we shall rest, until time and circumstances lead you to push the investigation farther. I have in me little of the spirit of proselytism. A mere abstract opinion, supposing it not to affect the conduct or disposition of him who holds it, would be in my eyes of very minor importance. And it is only in so far as I believe that all our opinions, however apparently removed from any practical consequences, do always more or less affect one or the other — our conduct or our dispositions — that I am at the pains to correct in my scholars, those which appear to me erroneous. I understand you to say, that to enter upon the discussion of certain opinions, which you consider as sacred truths, would appear to argue a doubt of those truths, and that a doubt would here constitute a crime. Now as I think such a belief inconsistent with candor and charity — two feelings, indispensable both for the enjoyment of happiness ourselves, and for its distribution to others, I shall challenge its investigation. If the doubt of any truth shall constitute a crime, then the belief of the same truth should constitute a virtue."

"Perhaps a duty would rather express it."

"When you charge the neglect of any duty as a crime, or account its fulfillment a virtue, you suppose the existence of a power to neglect or fulfill; and it is the exercise of this power, in the one way or the other, which constitutes the merit or demerit. Is it not so?"

"Certainly."

"Does the human mind possess the power to believe or disbelieve, at pleasure, any truths whatsoever?"

"I am not prepared to answer: but I think it does, since it possesses always the power of investigation."

"But, possibly, not the will to exercise the power. Take care lest I beat you with your own weapons. I thought this very investigation appeared to you a crime."

"Your logic is too subtle," said the youth, "for my inexperience."

"Say rather, my reasoning too close. Did I bear you down with sounding words and weighty authorities, and confound your understanding with hair-drawn distinctions, you would be right to retreat from the battery."

"I have nothing to object to the fairness of your deductions," said Theon, "But would not the doctrine be dangerous that should establish our inability to help our belief; and might we not stretch the principle, until we asserted our inability to help our actions?"

"We might, and with reason. But we will not now traverse the ethical *pons asinorum* of necessity — the most simple and evident of moral truths, and the most darkened, tortured, and belabored by moral teachers. You inquire if the doctrine we have essayed to establish, be not dangerous. I reply — not, if it be true. Nothing is so dangerous as error, — nothing so safe as truth. A dangerous truth would be a contradiction in terms, and an anomaly in things."
"But what is a truth?" said Theon.

"It is pertinently asked. A truth I consider to be an ascertained fact; which truth would be changed into an error, the moment the fact, on which it rested, was disproved."
"I see, then, no fixed basis for truth."

"It surely has the most fixed of all — the nature of things. And it is only an imperfect insight into that nature, which occasions all our erroneous conclusions, whether in physics or morals."

"But where, if we discard the gods, and their will, as engraven on our hearts, are our guides in the search after truth ?"

"Our senses and our faculties as developed in and by the exercise of our senses, are the only guides with which I am acquainted. And I do not see why, even admitting a belief in the gods, and in a superintending providence, the senses should not be viewed as the guides, provided by them, for our direction and instruction. But here is the evil attendant on an ungrounded belief, whatever be its nature. The moment we take one thing for granted, we take other things for granted: we are started in a wrong road, and it is seldom that we can gain the right one, until we have trodden back our steps to the starting place. I know but of one thing that a philosopher should take for granted; and that only because he is forced to it by an irresistible impulse of his nature; and because, without doing so, neither truth nor falsehood could exist for him. He must take for granted the evidence of his senses; in other words, he must believe in the existence of things, as they exist to his senses. I *know* of no other existence, and can therefore *believe* in no other: although, reasoning from analogy, I may *imagine* other existences to be. This, for in stance, I do as respects the gods. I see around me, in the world I inhabit, an infinite variety in the arrangement of matter; — a multitude of sentient beings, possessing different kinds, and varying grades of power and intelligence, — from the worm that crawls in the dust, to the eagle that soars to the sun, and man who marks to the sun its course. It is possible, it is moreover probable, that, in the worlds which I see not, — in the boundless infinitude and eternal duration of matter, beings may exist, of every countless variety, and varying grades of intelligence inferior and superior to our own, until we descend to a minimum, and rise to a maximum, to which the range of our observation affords no parallel, and of which our senses are inadequate to the conception. Thus far, my young friend, I believe in the gods, or in what you will of existences removed from the sphere of my knowledge.

That you should believe, with positiveness, in one unseen existence or another, appears to me no crime, although it may appear to me unreasonable: and so, my doubt of the same should appear to you no moral offense, although you might account it erroneous. I fear to fatigue your attention, and will, therefore, dismiss, for the present, these abstruse subjects."

But we shall both be amply repaid for their discussion, if this truth remain with you — that an opinion, right or wrong, can never constitute a moral offense, nor be in itself a moral obligation. It may be mistaken; it may involve an absurdity, or a contradiction. It is a truth; or it is an error: it can never be a crime or a virtue."

CHAPTER XV.

Theon remained transfixed to the same spot of earth on which the sage left him. A confused train of thoughts traveled through his brain, which his reason sought in vain to arrest, or to analyze. At one moment it seemed as if a ray of light had dawned upon his mind, opening to it a world of discovery as interesting as it was novel. Then suddenly he started as from the brink of a precipice, whose depths were concealed in darkness." "Cleanthes then had justly expounded the doctrines of the garden. — But did these doctrines involve the delinquency which he had hitherto supposed? Were they inconsistent with reason, and irreconcilable with virtue? If so, I shall be able to detect their fallacy," said the youth, pursuing his soliloquy aloud. "It were a poor compliment to the truths I have hitherto worshiped, did I shrink from their investigation. And yet, to question the power of the gods! To question their very existence! To refuse the knee of homage to that great first cause of all things, that speaks, and breathes, and shines resplendent throughout all animated nature! To dispute I know not what — of truths, as self-evident as they are sacred; which speak to our eyes and to our ears: to those very senses whose testimony alone is without appeal in the garden!"

"Do you object to the testimony, young Corinthian?" said a voice, which Theon recognized as that of Metrodorus.

"You arrive opportunely," said Theon, "that is, if you will listen to the questions of my doubting and embarrassed mind."

"Say rather, if I can answer them."

"I attribute to you the ability," said Theon, "since I have heard you quoted as an able expounder of the philosophy of the garden."

"In the absence of our Zeno," said the scholar with a smile, "I sometimes play the part of his Cleanthes. And though you may find me less eloquent than my brother of the porch, I will promise equal fidelity to the text of my original. But here is one, who can expound the doctrine in the letter and the spirit; and, with such an assistant, I should not fear to engage all the scholars and all the masters in Athens."

"Nay, boast rather of thy cause than of thy assistant," said Leontium, approaching, and playfully tapping the shoulder of Metrodorus: "nor yet belie thy own talents, my brother. The Corinthian will smile at thy false modesty, when he shall have studied thy writings, and listened to thy logical discourses. I imagine," she continued, turning her placid gaze on the youth, "that you have hitherto listened to more declamation than reasoning. I might also say, to more sophistry, seeing that you have walked and talked in the Lyceum."

"Say rather, walked and listened."

"In truth and I believe it," she returned with a smile, "and would that your good sense in this, were more common; and that men would rest content with straining their ears, and forbear from submitting their understandings, or torturing those of their neighbors."

"It might seem strange," said Metrodorus, "that the pedantry of Aristotle should find so many imitators, and his dark sayings so many believers, in a city, too, now graced and enlightened by the simple language, and simple doctrines of an Epicurus. — But the language of truth is too simple for inexperienced ears. We start in search of knowledge, like the demigods of old in search of adventure, prepared to encounter giants, to scale mountains, to pierce into Tartarean gulfs, and to carry off our prize from the grip of some dark enchanter, invulnerable to all save to charmed weapons and deity-gifted assailants. To find none of all these things, but, in their stead, a smooth road through a pleasant country, with a familiar guide to direct our curiosity, and point out the beauties of the landscape, disappoints us of all exploit and all notoriety; and our vanity turns but too often from the fair and open champaigne, into error's dark labyrinths, where we mistake mystery for wisdom, pedantry for knowledge, and prejudice for virtue."

"I admit the truth of the metaphor," said Theon. "But may we not simplify too much as well as too little? May we not push investigation beyond the limits assigned to human reason, and, with a boldness approaching to profanity, tear, without removing, the veil which enwraps the mysteries of creation from our scrutiny?"

"Without challenging the meaning of the terms you have employed," said Metrodorus, "I would observe, that there is little danger of our pushing investigation too far. Unhappily the limits prescribed to us by our few and imperfect senses must ever cramp the sphere of our observation, as compared to the boundless range of things; and that even when we shall have strained and improved our senses to the uttermost. We trace an effect to a cause, and that cause to another cause, and so on, till we hold some few links of a chain, whose extent like the charmed circle, is without beginning as without end."

"I apprehend the difficulties," observed Leontium, "which embarrass the mind of our young friend. Like most aspirants after knowledge, he has a vague and incorrect idea of what he is pursuing, and still more, of what may be attained. In the schools you have hitherto frequented," she continued, addressing the youth, "certain images of virtue, vice, truth, knowledge, are presented to the imagination, and these abstract qualities, or we may call them, figurative beings, are made at once the objects of speculation and adoration. A law is laid down, and the feelings and opinions of men are predicated upon it; a theory is built, and all animate and inanimate nature is made to speak in its support; an hypothesis is advanced, and all the mysteries of nature are treated as explained. You have heard of, and studied various systems of philosophy; but real philosophy is opposed to all systems. Her whole business is observation; and the results of that observation constitute all her knowledge. She receives no truths, until she has tested them by experience; she advances no opinions, unsupported by the testimony of facts; she acknowledges no virtue, but that involved in beneficial actions; no vice, but that involved in actions hurtful to ourselves or to others. Above all, she advances no dogmas, — is slow to assert what is, — and calls nothing impossible. The science of philosophy is simply a science of observation, both as regards the world without us, and the world within; and, to advance in it, are requisite only sound senses, well developed and exercised faculties, and a mind free of prejudice. The objects she has in view, as regards the external world, are, first, to see things as they are, and secondly, to examine their structure, to ascertain their properties, and to observe their relations one to the other. — As respects the world within, or the philosophy of mind, she has in view, first, to examine our sensations, or the impressions of external things on our senses; which operation involves, and is involved in, the examination of those external things themselves: secondly, to trace back to our sensations, the first development of all our faculties; and again, from these sensations, and the exercise of our different faculties as developed by them, to trace the gradual formation of our moral feelings, and of all our other emotions: thirdly, to analyze all these our sensations, thoughts, and emotions, — that is, to examine the qualities of our own internal, sentient matter, with the same, and yet more, closeness of scrutiny, than we have applied to the examination of the matter that is without us finally, to investigate the justness of our moral feelings, and to weigh the merit and demerit of human actions; which is, in other words, to judge of their tendency to produce good or evil, — to excite pleasurable or painful feelings in ourselves or others. You will observe, therefore, that, both as regards the philosophy of physics, and the philosophy of mind, all is simply a process of investigation.

It is a journey of discovery, in which, in the one case, we commission our senses to examine the qualities of that matter, which is around us, and, in the other, endeavor, by attention to the varieties of our consciousness, to gain a knowledge of those qualities of matter which constitute our susceptibilities of thought and feeling."

"This explanation is new to me," observed Theon, "and I will confess, startling to my imagination. It is pure materialism!"

"You may so call it," rejoined Leontiurn, "But when you have so called it — what then? The question remains: is it true? or is it false?"

"I should be disposed to say — false, since it confounds all my preconceived notions of truth and error, of right and wrong."

"Of truth and error, of right and wrong, in the sense of *correct* or *incorrect* is, I presume, your meaning," said Leontium. "You do not involve moral rectitude or the contrary in a matter of opinion?"

"If the opinion have a moral or immoral

tendency I do," said the youth.

"A simple matter of fact can have no such tendency or ought not, if we are rational creatures."

"And would not, if we were always reasoning beings," said Metrodorus; "but as the ignorance and superstition which surround our infancy and youth, favor the development of the imagination at the expense of the judgment, we are ever employed in the coining of chimeras, rather than in the discovery of truths; and if ever the poor judgment make an effort to dispel these fancies of the brain, she is repulsed, like a sacrilegious intruder into religious mysteries."

"Until our opinions are made to rest on facts," said Leontium, "the error of our young friend — the most dangerous of all errors, being one of principle and involving many — must ever pervade the world. And it was because I suspected this leading misconception of the very nature — of the very end and aim of the science he is pursuing, that I attempted an explanation of what should be sought, and of what can alone be attained. In philosophy —

that is, in knowledge — inquiry is everything; theory and hypothesis are worse than nothing. Truth is but approved facts. Truth, then, is one with the knowledge of these facts. To shrink from inquiry, is to shrink from knowledge. And to prejudge an opinion as true or false, because it interferes with some preconceived abstraction we call vice or virtue, is as if we were to draw the picture of a man we had never seen, and then, upon seeing him, were to dispute his being the man in question, because unlike our picture."

"But if this opinion interfered with another, of whose truth we imagined ourselves certain."

"Then clearly, in one or the other, we are mistaken; and the only way to settle the difficulty is to examine and compare the evidences of both."

"But are there not some truths self-evident?"

"There are a few which we may so call. That is to say, there are some facts, which we admit upon the evidence of a simple sensation; as, for instance, that a whole is greater than its part; that two are more than one; which we receive immediately upon the testimony of our sense of sight or of touch."

"But are there no moral truths of the same nature?"

"I am not aware of any. Moral truth, resting entirely upon the ascertained consequences of actions, supposes a process of observation and reasoning."

"What call you, then, a belief in a presiding providence, and a great first cause?"

"A belief resting upon testimony; which belief will be true or false, according to the correctness or incorrectness of that testimony."

"Is it not rather a self-evident moral truth?"

"In my answer, I shall have to divide your question into two. First, it cannot be a moral truth, since it is not deduced from the consequences of human action. It can be simply a truth, that is, a fact. Secondly, it is not a self-evident truth, since it is not evident to all minds, and frequently becomes less and less evident, the more it is examined."

"But is not the existence of a first or creating cause demonstrated to our senses by all we see, and hear, and feel?"

"The existence of all that we see and hear and feel is demonstrated to our senses; and the belief we yield to this existence is immediate and irresistible, that is, intuitive. — The existence of the creating cause, that you speak of, is not demonstrated to our senses; and therefore the belief in it cannot be immediate and irresistible. I prefer the expression "creating" to "first" cause, because it seems to present a more intelligible meaning. When you shall have examined farther into the phenomena of nature, you will see, that there can be as little a first as a last cause."

"But there must be always a cause, producing an effect."

"Certainly; and so your cause, — creating all that we see and hear and feel — must itself have a producing cause, otherwise you are in the same difficulty as before."

"I suppose it a Being unchangeable and eternal, itself unproduced, and producing all things."

"Unchangeable it *may* be, — eternal it *must* be — since every thing is eternal."

"Every thing eternal?"

"Yes; that is, the elements composing all substances are, so far as we know and can reason, eternal, and in their nature unchangeable; and it is apparently only the different disposition of these eternal and unchangeable atoms that produces all the varieties in the substances constituting the great material whole, of which we form a part. Those particles, whose peculiar agglomeration or arrangement, we call a vegetable to-day, pass into, and form part of an animal to-morrow; and that animal again, by the falling asunder of its constituent atoms, and the different approximation and agglomeration of the same, — or, of the same with other atoms, — is transformed into some other substance presenting a new assemblage of qualities. To this simple exposition of the phenomena of nature (which, you will observe, is not *explaining* their wonders, for that is impossible, but only *observing* them,) we are led by the exercise of our senses. In studying the existences which surround us, it is clearly our business to use our eyes, and not our imaginations. To see things as they are, is all we should attempt, and is all that is possible to be done. Unfortunately, we can do but little even here, as our eyes serve us to see but a very little way. But, were our eyes better — were they so good as to enable us to observe all the arcana of matter, we could never acquire any other knowledge of them, than that they are as they are; — and, in knowing this, that is, in seeing every link in the chain of occurrences, we should know all that even an omniscient being could know. One astronomer traces the course of the sun round the earth, another imagines that of the earth round the sun. Some future improvements in science may enable us to ascertain which conjecture is the true one. We shall then have ascertained a fact, which fact may lead to the discovery of other facts, and so on. Until this plain and simple view of the nature of all science be generally received, all the advances we may make in it are comparatively as nothing. Until we occupy ourselves in examining, observing, and ascertaining, and not in *explaining,* we are idly and childishly employed. — With every truth we may discover we shall mix a thousand errors; and, for one matter of fact, we shall charge our brain with a thousand fancies. To this leading misconception of the real, and only possible object of philosophical inquiry, I incline to attribute all the modes and forms of human superstition. The vague idea that some mysterious cause not merely *precedes* but *produces* the effect we behold, occasions us to wander from the real object in search of an imaginary one. We see the sun rise in the east: instead of confining our curiosity to the discovery of the time and manner of its rising, and of its course in the heavens, we ask also — *why* does it rise? What *makes* it move? The more ignorant immediately conceive some Being spurring it through the heavens, with fiery steeds, on wheels of gold, while the more learned tell us of laws of motion, decreed by an almighty fiat, and sustained by an almighty will. Imagine the truth of both suppositions: in the one case, we should see the application of what we call physical power in the driver and the steeds followed by the motion of the sun, and in the other, an almighty volition followed by the motion of the sun. But, in either case, should we understand *why* the sun moved? — *why* or *how* its motion followed what we call the impulse of the propelling power, or the propelling volition? All that we could *then* know, more than we *now* know, would be, that the occurrence of the motion of the sun was preceded by another occurrence; and if we afterwards frequently observed the same sequence of occurrences, they would become associated in our mind as necessary precedent and consequent — as cause and effect: and we might give to them the appellation of law of nature, or any other appellation; but they would still constitute merely a truth — that is a *fact*, and envelope no other mystery, than that involved in every occurrence and every existence."

"But, according to this doctrine," said Theon, "there would be no less reason in attributing the beautiful arrangement of the material world to the motion of a horse, than to the volition of an almighty mind."

"If I saw the motion of a horse followed by the effect you speak of, I should believe in some relation between them; and if I saw it follow the volition of an almighty mind — the same."

"But the cause would be inadequate to the effect."

"It could not be so, if it were the cause. For what constitutes the adequacy of which you speak? Clearly only the contact, or immediate proximity of the two occurrences. If any sequence could in fact be more wonderful than another, it should rather seem to be for the consequent to impart grandeur to the precedent — the effect to the cause, — than for the cause to impart grandeur to the effect. But in reality all sequences are equally wonderful. That light should follow the appearance of the sun, is just as wonderful, and no more so, as if it were to follow the appearance of any other body — and did light follow the appearance of a black stone it would excite astonishment simply because we never saw light follow such an appearance before. Accustomed, as we now are, to see light when the sunrises, our wonder would be, if we did not see light when he rose : but were light regularly to attend the appearance of any other body, our wonder at such a sequence would, after a time, cease; and we should then say, as we now say, there is a light *because* such a body has risen; and imagine *then*, as we imagine *now*, that we understand why *light* is."

"In like manner all existences are equally wonderful. An African lion is in himself nothing more extraordinary than a Grecian horse; although the whole people of Athens will assemble to gaze on the lion, and exclaim how wonderful! while no man observes the horse."

"True — but this is the wondering of ignorance."

"I reply — true again, but so is all wondering. If, indeed, we should consider it in this and in all other cases as simply an emotion of pleasurable surprise, acknowledging the presence of a novel object, the feeling is perfectly rational; but if it imagine anything more intrinsically marvelous in the novel existence, than in the familiar one, it is then clearly the idle — that is, the unreasoned and unreflecting marveling of ignorance. There is but one real wonder to the thinking mind: it is the existence of all things; that is the existence of matter. And the only rational ground of this one great wonder is, that the existence of matter is the last link in the chain of cause and effect at which we can arrive. You imagine yet another link — the existence of a power creating that matter. — My only objections to this additional link, or superadded cause, are, that it is *imagined*, and that it leaves the wonder as before; unless, indeed, we should say that it has superadded other wonders, since it supposes a power, or rather, an existence possessing a power, of which we never saw an example."

"How so? Does not even man possess a species of creating power? And do you not suppose, in your inert matter, that very property which others attribute, with more reason it appears to me, to some superior and unknown existence?'"

"By no means. No existence, that we know of, possesses creating power, in the sense you suppose. Neither the existence we call a man, nor any other of the existences comprised under the generic names of matter, physical world, nature, &c., possesses the power of calling into being its own constituent elements, nor the constituent elements of any other substance. It can change one substance into another substance, by altering the position of its particles, or intermingling them with others: but it cannot call into being, any more than it can annihilate, those particles themselves. The hand of man causes to approach particles of earth and of water, and, by their approximation produces clay; to which clay it gives a regular form, and, by the application of fire, produces the vessel we call a vase. You may say that the hand of man creates the vase, but it does not create the earth, or the water, or the fire; neither has the admixture of these substances added to, or subtracted from, the sum of their elementary atoms. Observe, therefore, there is no analogy between the power inherent in matter, of changing its appearance and qualities, by a simple change in the position of its particles, and that which you attribute to some unseen existence, who by a simple volition, should have called into being matter itself, with all its wonderful properties. An existence possessing such a power I have never seen; and though this says nothing against the possibility of such an existence, it says every thing against *my belief* in it. And farther, the power which you attribute to this existence — that of willing every thing out of nothing, — being, not only what I have never seen, but. that of which I cannot with any distinctness conceive — it must appear to me the greatest of all improbabilities."

"Our young friend," observed Metrodorus, "lately made use of an expression, the error involved in which, seems to be at the root of his difficulty. In speaking of matter," he continued, turning to Theon, "you employed the epithet inert. What is your meaning? And what matter do you here designate?"

"All matter surely is, in itself, inert."

"All matter surely is, in itself, as it is," said Metrodorus with a smile; "and that, I should say, is living and active. Again, what is matter?"

"All that is evident to our senses," replied Theon, "and which stands opposed to mind."

"All matter then is inert which is devoid of mind. "What then do you understand by mind?"

"I conceive some error in my definition," said Theon, smiling. "Should I say — *thought* — you would ask if every existence devoid of thought was inert, or if every existence, possessing life, possessed thought."

"I should so have asked. Mind or thought I consider a quality of that matter constituting the existence we call a man, which quality we find in a varying degree in other existences; many, perhaps all animals, possessing it. Life is another quality, or combination of qualities, of matter, inherent in — we know not how many existences. We find it in vegetables; we might perceive it even in stones, could we watch their formation, growth, and decay. We may call that active principle, pervading the elements of all things, which approaches and separates the component particles of the ever-changing, and yet ever-enduring world — life. Until you discover some substance, which undergoes no change, you cannot speak of inert matter: it can only be so, at least, relatively, — that is, as compared with other substances."

"The classing of thought and life among the qualities of matter is new to me."

"What is in a substance cannot be separate from it. And is not all matter a compound of qualities? Hardness, extension, form, color, motion, rest — take away all these, and where is matter? To conceive of mind independent of matter, is as if we should conceive of color independent of a substance colored: What is form, if not a body of a particular shape? What is thought, if not something which thinks? Destroy the substance, and you destroy its properties; and so equally — destroy the properties, and you destroy the substance. To suppose the possibility of retaining the one, without the other, is an evident absurdity."

"The error of conceiving a quality in the abstract often offended me in the Lyceum," returned the youth, "but I never considered the error as extending to mind and life, any more than to vice and virtue."

"You stopped short with many others," said Leontium. "It is indeed surprising how many acute minds will apply a logical train of reasoning in one case, and invert the process in another exactly similar."

"To return, and if you will, to conclude our discussion," said Metrodorus, "I will observe that no real advances can be made in the philosophy of mind, without a deep scrutiny into the operations of nature, or material existences. Mind being only a quality of matter, the study we call the philosophy of mind, is necessarily only a branch of general physics, or the Study of a particular part of the philosophy of matter."

"I am indebted to your patience," said the youth, "and would fain intrude farther on it. I will confine myself at present, however, to one observation. The general view of things, which you present to my mind, the simplicity of which I will confess to be yet more fascinating than its novelty, is evidently unfavorable to religion, — and, if so, unfavorable to virtue."

"An opportunity will, to-day, be afforded you," said Leontium, "of examining this important question in detail. At the request of some of our youth, the Master will himself give his views on the subject."

"I am all curiosity," said Theon. "Other teachers have commanded my respect, inflamed my imagination, and, I believe, often controlled my reason. The son of Neocles inspires me with love, and wins me to confidence, by encouraging me to exercise my own judgment, in scanning his arguments, and examining the groundwork of his own opinions. With such a teacher, and in such a school, I feel suspicion to be wholly misplaced; and I shall now start in the road of inquiry, anxious only to discover truth, and willing to part with every erroneous opinion, the moment it shall be proved to be erroneous."

NOTE BY THE TRANSLATOR. — How beautifully have the modern discoveries in chemistry and natural philosophy, and the more accurate analysis of the human mind — sciences unknown to the ancient world — substantiated the leading principles of the Epicurean ethics and physics — the only ancient school of either, really deserving the name.

To what have all our ingenious inventions

and contrivances for the analysis of material substances led us, but to the atoms of Epicurus? To what, our accurate observation of the decomposition of substances, and the arresting and weighing of their most subtle and invisible elements, but to the eternal and unchangeable nature of those atoms? We have, in the course of our scrutiny, superadded to the wonderful qualities of matter with which he was acquainted, those which we call attraction, repulsion, electricity, magnetism, &c. How do these discoveries multiply and magnify the living powers inherent in the simple elements of all existences, and point our admiration to the sagacity of that intellect which 2,000 years ago, started in the true road of inquiry; while, at this day, thousands of teachers, and millions of scholars are stumbling in the paths of error!

If we look to our mental philosophy, to what has our scrutiny led, but to the leading principles of Epicurean ethics. In the pleasure, — utility, — propriety of human action — whatever word we employ, the meaning is the same — in the consequences of human actions, that is, in their tendency to promote our good or our evil, we must ever find the only test of their intrinsic merit or demerit.

It might seem strange that, while the truth of the leading principles of the Epicurean philosophy have been long admitted by all sound reasoners, the abuse of the school and of its founder is continued to this day: this might and would seem strange and incomprehensible, did we not, on every subject find the same cowardly fear effacing, openly and honestly, the prejudices of men. Teachers, aware of the ignorance of those they teach, develop their doctrines in language intelligible only to the few; or, where they hazard a more distinct exposition of truth, shelter themselves from obloquy by echoing the vulgar censure against those who have taught the same truth, with more explicitness, before them. The mass, even of what is called the educated world, know nothing of the principles they decry, or of the characters they abuse. It is easy, therefore, by joining in the abuse against the one, to encourage a belief that we cannot be advocating the other. This desire of standing fair with the wise, without incurring the enmity of the ignorant, may suit with the object of those who acquire knowledge only for its display, or for the gratification of mere curiosity. But they whose nobler aim, and higher gift it is, to advance the human mind in the discovery of truth, must stand proof equally to censure and to praise. That such lips and such pens should employ equivocation, or other artifice, to turn aside the wrath of ignorance, is degrading to themselves and mortifying to their admirers. The late amiable and enlightened teacher, Thomas Brown, of Edinburgh, whose masterly exposition of old and new truths, and exposure of modern as well as ancient errors, has so advanced the science he professed, is yet chargeable with this weakness. After inculcating the leading principles of the Epicurean philosophy, and building upon those principles, the whole of his beautiful system, he condescends to soothe the prejudices which all his arguments have tended to uproot, by passing a sweeping censure on the school, whose doctrines he has borrowed and taught. We might say — how unworthy of such a mind! But we will rather say — how is it to be lamented that such a mind bears not within itself the conviction that all truths are important to all men; and that to employ deception with the ignorant, is to defeat our *own purpose; which is, surely, not to open the eyes of those who already see, but to enlighten the blind!*

CHAPTER XVI.

A MORE than usual crowd attended the instructions of the sage. The gay, and the curious, the learned, and the idle, of all ages, and of either sex, from the restless population of the city; many citizens of note, collected from various parts of Attica; and no inconsiderable portion of strangers from foreign states and countries.

They were assembled on the lawn, surrounding the temple already frequently mentioned. The contracting waters of Ilyssus flowed nearly in their accustomed bed; and earth and air, refreshed by the storm of the preceding night, resisted the rays of the uncurtained sun, now climbing high in the heavens. A crowd of recollections rushed on the young mind of Theon, as he entered the beautiful enclosure, and gazed on the stream which formed one of its boundaries. His thoughts again played truant to philosophy, and his rapid glance sought another and a fairer form than any it found there, when the approach of Epicurus divided the throng, and hushed the loud murmur of tongues into silence. The sage passed on, and it was not till he ascended the marble steps, and turned to address the assembly, that Theon perceived he had been followed by the beautiful being who ruled his fancy. The hues of Hebe now dyed her lips and her cheeks; but the laughing smiles of the preceding evening were changed for the composure of respectful attention. Her eye caught that of Theon. She gave a blush and a smile of recognition. Then, seating herself at the base of a column to the right of her father, her face resumed its composure, and her full dark eyes fastened on the countenance of the sage, in a gaze of mingled admiration and filial love.

"Fellow-citizens, and fellow-men! We purpose, this day, to examine a question of vital importance to human kind: no less a one than the relations we bear to all the existences that surround us; the position we hold in this beautiful material world? the origin, the object, and the end of our being; the source from which we proceed, and the goal to which we tend. — This question embraces many. It embraces all most interesting to our curiosity, and influential over our happiness. Its correct or incorrect solution must ever regulate, as it now regulates, our rule of conduct, our conceptions of right and wrong; must start us on the road of true or false inquiry, and either open our minds to such a knowledge of the wonders working in and around us, as our senses and faculties can attain, or close them for ever with the bands of superstition, leaving us a prey to fear, the slaves of our ungoverned imaginations, wondering and trembling at every occurrence in nature, and making our own existence and destiny sources of dread and mystery."

"Ere we come to this important inquiry, it behooves us to see that we come with willing minds; that we say not, 'so far will we go and no farther; we will make one step, but not two; we will examine, but only so long as the result of our examination shall confirm our preconceived opinions.' In our search after truth, we must equally discard presumption and fear. We must come with our eyes and our ears, our hearts and our understandings open; anxious, not to find *ourselves* right, but to discover what *is* right; asserting nothing which we cannot prove; believing nothing which we have not examined; and examining all things fearlessly, dispassionately, perseveringly."

"In our preceding discourses, and, for such as have not attended these, in our writings, we have endeavored to explain the real object of philosophical enquiry; we have directed you to the investigation of nature, to all that you see of existences and occurrences around you; and we have shown that, in these existences and occurrences, all that *can* be known, and all that *there is* to be known, lies hid. We have exhorted you to use your eyes, and your judgments, never your imagination; to abstain from theory, and rest with facts; and to understand that in the accumulation of facts, as regards the nature and properties of substances, the order of occurrences, and the consequences of actions, lies the whole science of philosophy, physical and moral. We have seen, in the course of our enquiry, that in matter itself exist all causes and effects; that the eternal particles, composing all substances are, so far as we know and can reason, eternal, and in their nature unchangeable; and it is apparently only the different disposition of these eternal and unchangeable atoms that produces all the varieties in the substances constituting the great material whole, of which we form a part. Those particles, whose peculiar agglomeration or arrangement, we call a vegetable to-day, pass into, and form part of an animal to-morrow; and that animal again, by the falling asunder of its constituent atoms, and the different approximation and agglomeration of the same, — or, of the same with other atoms, — is transformed into some other substance presenting a new assemblage of qualities. To this simple exposition of the phenomena of nature (which, you will observe, is not *explaining* their wonders, for that is impossible, but only *observing* them,) we are led by the exercise of our senses. In studying the existences which surround us, it is clearly our business to use our eyes, and not our imaginations. To see things as they are, is all we should attempt, and is all that is possible to be done. We have seen, in the course of our inquiry, that in matter itself exist all causes and effects; that the eternal particles, composing all substances, form the first and last links in the chain of occurrences, or of cause and effect, at which we can arrive; that the qualities, inherent in these particles, produce, or are followed by, certain effects; that the changes, in position, of these particles, produce or are followed by certain other qualities and effects; that the sun appears, and that light follows his appearance; that we throw a pearl into vinegar, and that the pearl vanishes from our eyes, to assume the form or forms of more subtle, but not less real substances; that the component particles of a human being fall asunder, and that, instead of a man, we find a variety of other substances or existences, presenting new appearances, and new properties or powers; that a burning coal touches our hand, that the sensation of pain follows the contact, that the desire to end this sensation is the next effect in succession, and that the muscular motion of withdrawing the hand, following the desire, is another. That in all this succession of existences and events, there is nothing but what we see, or what we could see, if we had better eyes; that there is no mystery in nature, but that involved in the very existence of all things; and that things being as they are is no more wonderful than it would be if they were different. That an analogous course of events, or chain of causes and effects, takes place in morals as in physics; that is to say, in examining those qualities, of the matter composing our own bodies, which we call mind, we can only trace a train of occurrences, in like manner as we do in the external world; that our sensations, thoughts, and emotions, are simply effects following causes, a series of consecutive phenomena, mutually producing and produced."

"When we have taken this view of things, observe how all abstruse questions disappear; how all science is simplified; all knowledge rendered easy and familiar to the mind! Once started in this only true road of inquiry, every step we make is one in advance. To whatever science we apply, that is, to whatever part of matter, or to whichever of its qualities, we direct our attention, we shall, in all probability, make important, because true, discoveries. It is the philosophy of nature in general, or any one of those subdivisions of it, which we call the philosophy of Mind, Ethics, Medicine, Astronomy, Geometry, &c., the moment we occupy ourselves in observing and arranging in order the facts, which are discovered in the course of observation, we acquire positive knowledge, and may safely undertake to develop it to others."

"The ascertaining the nature of existences, the order of occurrences, and the consequences of human actions constituting, therefore, the whole of knowledge, what is there to prevent each and all of us from extending our discoveries to the full limits prescribed by the nature of our facilities and duration of our existence? What nobler employment can we invent? What pleasure so pure, so little liable to disappointment? What is there to hold us back? What is there not to spur us forward? Does our ignorance start from the very simplicity of knowledge? Do we fear to open our eyes lest we should see the light? Does the very truth we seek alarm us in its attainment? — How is it that, placed in this world as on a theatre of observation, surrounded by wonders and endowed with faculties wherewith to scan these wonders, we know so little of what is, and imagine so much of what is not? Other animals, to whom man accounts himself superior, exercise the faculties they possess, trust their testimony, follow the impulses of their nature, and enjoy the happiness of which they are capable. Man alone, the most gifted of all known existences, doubts the evidence of his superior senses, perverts the nature and uses of his multiplied faculties, controls his most innocent, as well as his noblest impulses, and to poison all the sources of his happiness. To what are we to trace this fatal error, this cruel self-martyrdom, this perversion of things from their natural bent? In the over-development of one faculty and neglect of another, we must seek the cause. In the imagination, that source of our most beautiful pleasures when under the control of judgment, we find the source of our worst afflictions."

"From an early age, I have made the nature and condition of man my study. I have found him in many countries of the earth, under the influence of all varieties of climate and circumstance; I have found him the savage lord of the forest, clothed in the rough skins of animals less rude than himself, sheltered in the crevices of the mountains and caves of the earth from the blasts of winter and heats of the summer sun; I have found him the slave of masters debased as himself, crouching to the foot that spurns him, and showing no signs of miscalled civilization but its sloth and its sensualities. I have found him the lord over millions, clothed in purple and treading courts of marble; the cruel destroyer of his species, marching through blood and rapine, to thrones of extended dominion; the iron-hearted tyrant, feasting on the agonies of his victims, and wringing his treasure from the hard-earned mite of industry; I have found him the harmless but ignorant tiller of the soil, eating the simple fruits of his labor, sinking to rest only to rise again to toil, toiling to live and living only to die; I have found him the polished courtier, the accomplished scholar, the gifted artist, the creating genius; the fool and the knave; rich and a beggar; spuming and spurned."

"Under all these forms and varieties of the external and internal man, still, with hardly an exception, I have found him unhappy. With more capacity for enjoyment than any other creature, I have seen him surpassing the rest of existences only in suffering and crime. "Why is this and from whence? A master error, for some there must be, leads to results so fatal — so opposed to the apparent nature and promise of things? Long have I sought this error — this main-spring of human folly and human crime. I have traced, through all their lengthened train of consequents and causes, human practice and human theory; I have threaded the labyrinth to its dark beginning; I have found the first link in the chain of evil; I have found it — in all countries

— among all tribes and tongues and nations; I have found it, — fellow-men, I have found it in — RELIGION!"

A low murmur here rose from one part of the assembly. A deep and breathless silence succeeded. The sage turned his gaze slowly around, and with a countenance, pure and serene as the skies which shone above him, proceeded.

"We have named the leading error of the human mind, — the bane of human happiness — the perverter of human virtue! It is Religion — that dark coinage of trembling ignorance! It is Religion — that prisoner of human felicity! It is Religion —that blind guide of human reason. It is Religion — that dethroner of human virtue! -which lies at the root of all the evil and all the misery that pervade the world!"

"Not hastily formed, still less hastily expressed, has been the opinion you hear this day. A long train of reflection led to the discarding of religion as an error, a life of observation to the denouncing it as an evil. In considering it as devoid of truth, I am but one of many. Few have looked deeply and steadily into the nature of things and not called in question belief in existences unseen and causes unknown. But while smiling at the credulity of their fellow-beings, philosophers have thought reason good only for themselves. They have argued that religion, however childish a chimera in itself, was useful in its tendencies: that, if it rested upon nothing, it supported all things; that it was the stay of virtue, and the source of happiness. However opposed to every rule in philosophy, physical and moral; however apparently in contradiction to reason and common sense that a thing untrue could be useful; that a belief in facts disproved or unproved could afford a sustaining prop to a just rule of practice; the assertion came supported by so universal a testimony of mankind, and by individual names of such authority in practical wisdom and virtue, that I hesitated to call it mistaken. And as human happiness appeared to me the great desideratum, and its promotion the only object consistent with the views of a teacher of men, I forbore from all expression of opinion, until I had fully substantiated, to my own conviction, both its truth and its tendency.

The *truth* of my opinion is substantiated, as we have seen, by an examination into the nature of things; that is, into the properties of matter, which are alone sufficient to produce all the chances and changes that we behold. Its *tendency* is discovered by an examination into the moral condition of man."

"The belief in supernatural existences, and the expectation of a future life, are said to be sources of happiness, and stimuli to virtue. How, and in what way? Is it proved by experience? Look abroad over the earth; everywhere the song of praise, the prayer of supplication, the smoke of incense, the blow of sacrifice, arise from forest, and lawn, from cottage, palace, and temple, to the gods of human idolatry. Religion, is spread over the earth. If she be the parent of virtue and happiness, they too should cover the earth. Do they so? Read the annals of human tradition! Go forth and observe the actions of men! Who shall speak of virtue — who of happiness, that hath eyes to see and ears to hear and hearts to feel? No! experience is against the assertion. The world is full of religion, and full of misery and crime."

"Can the assertion be sustained by argument, by any train of reasoning whatsoever? Imagine a Deity under any fashion of existence; how are our dreams concerning him in an imaginary heaven to affect our happiness or our conduct on a tangible earth? Affect it indeed they may for evil, but how for good? The idea of an unseen Being, ever at work around and about us, may afflict the human intellect with idle terrors, but can never guide the human practice to what is rational and consistent with our nature. Grant that, by any possibility, we could ascertain the existence of one god, or of a million of gods: we see them not, we hear them not, we feel them not. Unless they were submitted to our observation, were fashioned like unto us, had similar desires, similar faculties, a similar organization, how could their mode of existence afford a guide for ours? As well should the butterfly take pattern from the lion, or the lion from the eagle, as man from a god. To say nothing of the inconsistency of the attributes, with which all gods are decked, it is enough that none of them are ours. We are men; they are gods. They inhabit other worlds; we inhabit the earth. Let them enjoy their felicity; and let us, my friends, seek ours."

"But it is not that religion is merely useless, it is mischievous. It is mischievous by its idle terrors; it is mischievous by its false morality; it is mischievous by its hypocrisy; by its fanaticism; by its dogmatism; by its threats; by its hopes; by its promises. Consider it under its mildest and most amiable form, it is still mischievous, as inspiring false motives of action, as holding the human mind in bondage, and diverting the attention from things useful, to things useless. The essence of religion is fear, as its source is ignorance. In a certain stage of human knowledge, the human mind must of necessity, in its ignorance of the properties of matter, and its dark insight into the chain of phenomena arising out of those properties — must of necessity reason falsely on every occurrence and existence in nature; it must of necessity, in the absence of fact, give the rein to fancy, see a miracle in every uncommon event, and imagine unseen agents as producing all that it beholds. In proportion as the range of our observation is enlarged, and that we learn to connect and arrange the phenomena of nature, we curtail our list of miracles, and the number of our supernatural agents. An eclipse is alarming to the vulgar, as denoting the wrath of offended deities; to the man of science it is a simple occurrence, as easily traced to its cause as any the most familiar to our observation. The knowledge of one generation is the ignorance of the next. Our superstitions decrease as our attainments multiply; and the fervor of our religion declines as we draw nearer to the conclusion which destroys it entirely. That conclusion, based upon accumulated facts, is as we have seen, that matter alone is at once the thing acting, and the thing acted upon, — eternal in duration, infinitely various and varying in appearance: never diminishing in quantity, and always changing in form. Without some knowledge of what is styled natural philosophy, or physics, no individual can attain this conclusion. And in a *certain* stage of that knowledge, more or less advanced according to the acuteness of the intellect, it will be impossible for any individual, not mentally obtuse, to shun that conclusion. This truth is one of infinite importance. The moment we consider the hostility directed against what is called Atheism, as the natural result of deficient information, the mind must be diseased which could resent that hostility. And perhaps a simple statement of the truth would best lead to examination of the subject, and to the conversion of mankind.

"Imagine this conversion, my friends! Imagine the creature man in the full exercise of all his faculties; not shrinking from knowledge, but eager in its pursuit; not bending the knee of adulation to visionary beings armed by fear for his destruction, but standing erect in calm contemplation of the beautiful face of nature; discarding prejudice, and admitting truth without fear of consequences; acknowledging no judge but reason, no censor but that in his own breast! Thus considered, he is transformed into the god of his present idolatry, or rather into a far nobler being, possessing all the attributes consistent with virtue and reason, and none opposed to either. How great a contrast with his actual state! His best faculties dormant; his judgment unawakened within him; his very senses misemployed; all his energies misdirected; trembling before the coinage of his own idle fancy; seeing over all creation a hand of tyranny extended; and instead of following virtue, worshiping power!

Monstrous creation of ignorance! monstrous degradation of the noblest of known existences! Man, boasting of superior reason, of moral discrimination, imagines a being at once unjust, cruel, and inconsistent; then, kissing the dust, calls himself its slave! "This world *is*," says the theist, "therefore it was made." — By whom? — "By a being more powerful than I." Grant this infantine reasoning, what follows as the conclusion? "That we must fear him," says the theist. — And why? Is his power directed against our happiness? Does your god amuse himself by awakening the terrors of more helpless beings? Fear him then indeed we may; and, let our conduct be what it will, fear him we *must*. "He is good as well as powerful," says the theist; "therefore the object of love," — How do we ascertain his goodness? I see indeed a beautiful and curious world; but I see it full of moral evils, and presenting many physical imperfections. Is he all-powerful? perfect good or perfect evil might exist. Is he all-powerful *and* all-good? perfect good *must* exist. Of the sentient beings comprised in the infinity of matter I know but those which I behold. I set no limits to the number of those which I behold not; no bounds to their power.

One or many may have given directions to the elementary atoms, and may have fashioned this earth as the potter fashions its clay. Beings possessing such power may exist, and may have exercised it. *All*-powerful still they are not, or being so they are wicked: *evil exists.* I know not what may be — but this my moral sense tells me cannot be — a fashioner of the world I inhabit, in his nature all-good and all-powerful. I see yet another impossibility; a fashioner of this world in his nature all-good and *fore-knowing.* Granting the possibility of the attributes, their united existence were an impossible supposition in the architect of our earth."

"Let us accord his goodness the most pleasing and valuable attribute. Your god is then the object of our love, and of our pity. Of our love, because being benevolent in his own nature, he must have intended to produce happiness in forming ours; of our pity, because we see that he has failed in his intention. I cannot conceive a condition more unfortunate than that of a deity contemplating this world of his creation. Is he the author of some — say, of much happiness? of what untold misery is he not equally the author? I cannot conceive a being more desperately — more hopelessly wretched than that we have now pictured. The worst of human miseries shrink into comparative insignificancy before those of their author. How must every sigh drawn from the bosom of man rend the heart of his god! How must every violence committed on earth convulse the peace of heaven! unable to alter what he had fashioned, how must he equally curse his power and his impotence! And in bewailing our existence, how must he burn to annihilate his own!"

"We will now suppose his power without limit; and his knowledge extending to the future, as to the past. How monstrous the conception! What demon drawn from the fevered brain of insanity ever surpassed this deity in malignity! Able to make perfection, he hath sown through all nature the seed of evil. The lion pursues the lamb; the vulture, in his rage, tears the dove from her nest. Man, the universal enemy, triumphs even in the sufferings of his fellow-beings; in their pain finds his own joy; in their loss, his gain; in the frenzy of his violence, working out his own destruction; in the folly of his ignorance, cursing his own race, and blessing its cruel author! Your deity is the author of evil, and you call him good; the inventor of misery, and you call him happy! What virtuous mind shall yield homage to such a Being? Who shall say that homage, if tendered, degrades not the worshiper? Or, who shall say that homage, when rendered, shall pacify the idol? Will abjectness in the slave ensure mercy in the tyrant? Or, if it should, my friends, which of us would be the abject? Are men found bold to resist earthly oppression, and shall they bow before injustice because she speak from heaven? Does the name of Harmodius inspire our songs? Do crowns of laurel bind the temples of Aristogiton? Let our courage rise higher than theirs, my friends; and, if worthy of ambition, our fame! Dethrone, not the tyrant of Athens, but the tyrant of the earth! — not the oppressor of Athenians but the oppressor of mankind! Stand forth! Stand erect! Say to this god, 'if you made us in malice, we will not worship you in fear. We will judge of you by your works: and judge your works with our reason. If evil pervade them, you are chargeable with it as their author. We care not to conciliate your injustice, any more than to strive with your

power. We judge of the future from the past.
And as you have disposed of us in this world,
so, if it please you to continue our being must
you dispose of us in another. It would be idle
to strive with Omnipotence, or to provide
against the decrees of Omniscience. We will
not torment ourselves by imagining your
intentions; nor debase ourselves by
expostulations. Should you punish, in us, the
evil you have made, you will punish it as
unjustly as you made it maliciously. Should
you reward in us the good, you will reward it
absurdly, as it was equally your work, and
not ours.' "

"Let us now concede in argument the union of
all the enumerated attributes. Let us accord
the existence of a being perfect in goodness,
wisdom, and power, who shall have made all
things by his volition, and decreed all
occurrences in his wisdom. Such a being
must command our admiration and approval:
he can command no more. As he is good and
wise, he is superior to all praise; as he is great
and happy, he is independent of all praise. As
he is the author of our happiness, he has
ensured our love; but as he is our creator, he
may command from us no duties. Supposing

a god, all duties rest with him. If he has made us, he is bound to make us happy; and failing in the duty, he must be an object of just abhorrence to all his sentient creation. Kindness received must necessarily inspire affection. This kindness, in a divine creator, as in an earthly parent, is a solemn duty, — a sacred obligation, — the nonperformance of which were the most atrocious of crimes. When performed, love from the creature, as from the child, is a necessary consequence, and an all-sufficient reward."

"Allowing then to the theist his god, we stand to him in no relation that can inspire fear, or involve duty. He can give us no happiness that he was not bound to bestow: he can cherish us with no tenderness, that he was not bound to yield. It is for him to gratify all our desires, — or, if they be erroneous, to correct them. It is for us to demand every good in his power to grant, or in ours to enjoy. Let then, the theologist banish fear and duty from his creed. It is love — love alone that can be claimed by gods or yielded by men."

"Have we said enough? Surely the absurdity of all the doctrines of religion, and the iniquity of many, are sufficiently evident. To fear a being on account of his power, is degrading; to fear him if he be good, ridiculous. Prove to us his existence, and prove to us his perfections; prove to us his parental care; love springs up in our bosoms, and repays his bounty. If he care not to show us his existence, he desires not the payment of our love, and finds in the contemplation of his own works their reward."

"But, says the theist, his existence is evident — and, not to acknowledge it a crime. It is not so to me, my friends. I see no sufficient evidence of his existence: and to reason of its possibility, I hold to be an idle speculation. To doubt that which is evident is not in our power. To believe that which is not evident, is equally impossible to us. Theist! thou makest of thy god a being more weak, more silly, than thyself. He punisheth as a crime the doubt of his existence! Why, then, let him declare his existence, and we doubt no more. Should the wandering tribes of Scythia doubt the existence of Epicurus, should Epicurus be angry? What vanity — what absurdity — what silliness, O theists! do ye not suppose in your God! Let him exist, this god, in all the perfection of a poet's imagery; I lift to him a forehead assured and serene. I see thee, O God! in thy power, and admire thee: I see thee in thy goodness, and approve thee. Such homage only is worthy of thee to receive, or of me to render.' And what does he reply? 'Thou art right, creature of my fashioning! Thou canst not add to, nor take away from the sum of my felicity. I made thee to enjoy thy own, not to wonder at mine. I have placed thee amid objects of desire, I have given thee means of enjoyment. Enjoy, then! Be happy! It was for that I made thee.'"

"Hearken, then, my children! hearken to your teacher! Let it be a god or a philosopher who speaks, the injunction is the same: *Enjoy, and be happy!* Is life short? It is an evil: but render life happy, its shortness is the *only* evil. I call to you, as, if he exist, God must call to you from heaven: *Enjoy, and be happy!* Do you doubt the way? Let Epicurus be your guide. The source of every enjoyment is within yourselves. Good and evil lie before you. The good is — all which can yield you pleasure: the evil — what must bring you pain. Here is no paradox, no dark saying, no moral hid in tables."

"We have considered the unsound fabric of religion. It remains to consider that, equally unsound, of morals. The virtue of man is false as his faith. What folly invented, knavery supports. Let us arise in our strength, examine, judge, and be free!"

The teacher here paused. The crowd stood, as if yet listening.

"At a convenient season, my children, we will examine farther into the nature of man, and the science of life."

Study Guide

Chapter 1. What is the origin of Theon's prejudice and indignation?

Chapter 2. What are the possible dangers of intellectual arrogance? Should the vicious be pitied, seen with indignation, or contempt? Metrodorus' brother, Timocrates, had studied under Epicurus and then set about defaming him unfairly. What would be a philosopher's most appropriate response to this?

Chapter 3. How is Stoic virtue different from Epicurean virtue?

Chapter 4. Study the beliefs and lifestyles of members of the ancient philosophical school of the Cynics. Do you consider them extreme or impractical? What does Epicurus mean when he explains that producing great men is not the same as producing happy men? Can ambition be a virtue, and under which criteria?

Chapter 5. Why do the other schools argue that virtue can not be connected with pleasure? In what way do they understand pleasure, and how the Epicureans understand it?

Chapter 6. What is the most wise and practical way to publicly criticize what is reprehensible?

Chapter 7. Epicurus says he accepts men as they are, not as we would like them to be, and that his philosophy brings healing and happiness to men. In addition, his philosophy is for everyone, not just philosophers. How does this contrast with Stoicism? This chapter contains musings on the future decline of Hellenistic philosophies. What aspects of antiquity was the author trying to recover when she wrote this book in the nineteenth century?

Chapter 8. Note how in the story of Cleanthes, we see a comparison between the discipline and austerity of the Stoics versus Epicurean pleasure and ease. In what way is openness and frank speech an essential quality of a good philosopher? What effects does frank speech have in the role played by a philosopher in society, and in people's opinions of philosophers as a result of frank speech?

Chapter 9. How do the arts contribute to a happy life? What about science? And the other professions and skills?

Chapter 10. List the benefits, limitations and uses of therapeutic philosophy described here.

Chapter 11. Epicurus and Theon talk about how the wise will be remembered by those who appreciate wisdom. How would you describe a life well lived?

Chapter 12. List Hedea's points of criticism of the Pythagorean school.

Chapter 13. Should belief in gods and in divine providence be beyond reproach? How do we explain that these beliefs enjoy the privilege they enjoy in almost all societies?

Chapter 14. Throughout its history, the Epicurean tradition has always emphasized the importance of science and the objective study of the nature of the things perceived through our senses. List some of the reasons why this is important. What constitutes an open mind, and why is it important to cultivate?

Chapter 15. Philosophers here speak of the use of words, of how truth can be express in simple and clear terms, and of how truth does not need to be adorned with vague and mysterious talk. How does this aspect of Epicureanism contrast with other philosophies and religions? Leontion says that you should always reason from observation. What are the potential dangers of rationalism when it is not informed by our senses and faculties?

Leontion also says that there are no self-evident moral truths; that observation and reasoning are needed to identify the consequences of actions. This is called utilitarian hedonism. Study this philosophical tradition and write, in your own words, what its doctrine consists of and if it has merit.

Chapter 16. Wright's Epicurus regrets that man calls into question the power of his senses and poisons the sources of his happiness, and he criticizes the imagination as dangerous. What are proper uses for the imagination, and what are not?

Consider several specific historical events related to religion (say: the Crusades, the invasion of the Americas by Europeans, the persecution of scientists by the church, moments of recent terrorism, holy wars, etc.) You can also refer to statistics on living standards of the most religious societies versus the less religious ones. Do you think the severe criticism of religion in this chapter is deserved, in light of these specific events or empirical data?

The novel ends with an exhortation to happiness, whether we are secular or religious. What can be said of the peculiar expression of secular humanism we see in the Epicurean tradition? In what way does it differ from other forms of humanism?

Also, consider that the author was a friend of Thomas Jefferson, the author of the Declaration of Independence of the United States, who wrote into it that the pursuit of happiness is inherent to the human condition. It is known that Jefferson walked around with copies of parts of this work with him for many years. What can you say about the effect that this work, and Epicurean tradition in general, likely had in the history of the New World and of Western civilization?

48537412R00154

Made in the USA
Lexington, KY
04 January 2016